THE REVIEWS ARE IN FOR
DAN KENNEDY'S REVOLUTIONARY BOOK!

"Creative, intelligent, thought-provoking."
— Bill Foster, chairman of the board, Basketball Hall of Fame

"Kennedy's advice for success in business—and in life—goes against almost everything I've been taught. Overcoming my skepticism to follow his advice has enabled me to double my already successful company's profits in less than two years, with less effort, time, and stress on my part."
— Pamela Yellen, CEO, Prospecting and Marketing Institute, Inc., and co-author of *Zero Resistance Selling*

"Scores of new and fresh approaches to achieving success in an ever-changing world."
— Nido Qubein, past president, National Speakers Association

"Encourages readers who want to succeed to forget everything they ever heard about positive thinking, customer service, persistence, and more." — *Orange County Register*

"Kennedy offers counterintuitive advice in a lively, easy-to-read style. It just might give some people the necessary nudge to earn a few million dollars or at least a few hundred thousand."
— *Publishers Weekly*

"Kennedy's campaign to debunk common business myths succeeds." — *Booklist*

"Kennedy thumbs his nose at conventional paths to success. He maintains that even without a talent for creativity, pleasing personality, professional credentials, forced positive thinking, high IQ, or a natural-born anything, you can get that job."
— *Library Journal*

"My favorite new book for entrepreneurs. A quick read with lots of empowering stories. Entrepreneurs are constantly testing their limits; this book is an excellent tool for doing just that."
— *Minneapolis Star-Tribune*

DAN S. KENNEDY is a direct-marketing consultant and produces TV infomercials. As a popular professional speaker, he addresses over 200,000 people every year, sharing the platform with people like President George Bush, General Norman Schwarzkopf, General Colin Powell, and Zig Ziglar. He is the author of *How to Make Millions with Your Ideas* (Plume).

MYTHS & LIES

1. *"Think positive!" and life will be wonderful.* (page 1) Call me, I have some swampland to sell you.

2. *"Be pure of heart" and good things will come to you.* (page 6) So how come so many mean, nasty, intimidating, and manipulative folks seem to do so well?

3. *He's a born salesman.* (page 11) Really? Did he come out of the womb with a cell phone in one hand, briefcase in the other?

4. *You can't get anywhere these days without a college degree.* (page 18) Except to the top.

5. *The meek shall inherit the earth.* (page 27) But not in the foreseeable future.

6. *Modesty is a virtue.* (page 27) Tell Madonna.

7. *Mind your manners.* (page 35) But the barbarians are past the gate.

8. *Be original.* (page 55) Unless you want to get very rich, very fast—then copy like crazy.

9. *If at first you don't succeed, try, try again.* (page 64) Maybe not. Persistence isn't all it's cracked up to be.

10. *Keep your nose to the grindstone.* (page 64) And you'll have a very smooth, hard nose. And an aching back.

11. *Practice makes perfect.* (page 71) NOT!

12. *Winners never quit, quitters never win.* (page 74) Quit! The first step to getting out of a hole is to stop digging.

13. *Luck has nothing to do with success.* (page 90) Unless you're lucky.

14. *Haste makes waste.* (page 93) But "slow and steady" seems to be winning fewer and fewer races these days.

15. *Never mix business with pleasure.* (page 98) Hey, what kind of dull, boring, unpleasant advice is that?

16. *In business "the customer is always right."* (page 111) Some customers are damned nuisances and that's all there is to it.

17. *You can't "get rich quick."* (page 118) How are you doing with the get-rich-slow plan?

18. *It takes money to make money.* (page 125) Unless you haven't got any.

19. *Build a better mousetrap and the world will beat a path to your door.* (page 134) But don't hold your breath.

20. *Managers should treat everybody fairly.* (page 157) Unless the manager wants to achieve maximum productivity.

21. *If it ain't broke, don't fix it.* (page 166) And with that theory, we'd all be lighting our homes and offices with bigger candles.

FORGET EVERYTHING YOU'VE EVER BEEN TOLD ABOUT . . .

- Positive Thinking
- Pleasing Personality
- Formal Education
- Professional Credentials
- Creativity
- Expert Advice
- Customer Service
- Quality and Excellence
- Persistence

NO RULES

*21 Giant Lies About
Success and How to Make
It Happen Now*

(previously published as
*How to Succeed in Business by Breaking All the Rules:
A Plan for Entrepreneurs*)

Dan S. Kennedy

Foreword by Scott DeGarmo,
former editor in chief of *Success* magazine

A PLUME BOOK

PLUME
Published by the Penguin Group
Penguin Putnam Inc., 375 Hudson Street,
New York, New York 10014, U.S.A.
Penguin Books Ltd, 27 Wrights Lane,
London W8 5TZ, England
Penguin Books Australia Ltd, Ringwood,
Victoria, Australia
Penguin Books Canada Ltd, 10 Alcorn Avenue,
Toronto, Ontario, Canada M4V 3B2
Penguin Books (N.Z.) Ltd, 182–190 Wairau Road,
Auckland 10, New Zealand

Penguin Books Ltd, Registered Offices:
Harmondsworth, Middlesex, England

Published by Plume, an imprint of Dutton NAL,
a member of Penguin Putnam Inc.
Previously published in a Dutton edition under the title *How to Succeed in Business by Breaking All the Rules: A Plan for Entrepreneurs.*

First Plume Printing, September, 1998
10 9 8 7 6 5 4 3 2 1

Ⓟ REGISTERED TRADEMARK—MARCA REGISTRADA
Library of Congress Cataloging-in-Publication Data is available.

Printed in the United States of America

PUBLISHER'S NOTE
This publication is designed to provide accurate and authoritative information in regard to the subject matter covered. It is sold with the understanding that the publisher is not engaged in rendering financial, accounting, or other professional service. If financial advice or other expert assistance is required, the service of a competent professional person should be sought.

BOOKS ARE AVAILABLE AT QUANTITY DISCOUNTS WHEN USED TO PROMOTE PRODUCTS OR SERVICES. FOR INFORMATION PLEASE WRITE TO PREMIUM MARKETING DIVISION, PENGUIN PUTNAM INC., 375 HUDSON STREET, NEW YORK, NEW YORK 10014.

CONTENTS

Foreword by Scott DeGarmo   xi

Author's Introduction   xv

Chapter 1. Forget Just About Everything You Were
  Ever Told About Positive Thinking and Motivation   1

Chapter 2. The Myth of the Born Salesman.
  Or Born Anything.   11

Chapter 3. "You Can't Get Anywhere These Days
  Without a College Education."   18

Chapter 4. Modesty and Humility May Be Admirable
  Qualities in a Monk, but Not in an Entrepreneur   27

Chapter 5. "Mind Your Manners"—or Is Being Rude,
  Aggressive, Rough-Around-the-Edges One of the
  Great Unsung Secrets of Success?   35

Chapter 6. A Pox on Creativity   55

Chapter 7. Forget (Almost) Everything You've
Ever Been Told About Persistence   64

Chapter 8. All the Investment Advice You Can Get
May Be Worse Than No Investment Advice at All   78

Chapter 9. A Few More Success Myths
Blown to Bits, in Brief   90

Chapter 10. Special Contrarian Advice for
Young People—and Useful to Others   103

Chapter 11. When a Dog Bites You, Do You Have to Say
"Thank You, Nice Doggie"?   111

Chapter 12. Warning: You Can't Get Rich Quick—
or Can You?   118

Chapter 13. "It Takes Money to Make Money."   125

Chapter 14. Can It Be That the Product Doesn't
Matter All That Much?   134

Chapter 15. The Illusions of "Marketing"   141

Chapter 16. The Illusions of "Management"   151

Chapter 17. "If It Ain't Broke, Don't Fix It"
—Unless You Want To   166

Chapter 18. Some of My Favorite Contrarians   174

Author's Afterword   183

Acknowledgments, Notices,
Communication with the Author   185

Other Books by the Author   186

FOREWORD

Hooray! Here is a book that is: (1) fun to read, (2) incredibly motivating and inspiring, and (3) quite profound. In short, Dan Kennedy has broken the rules in terms of how much value an author can deliver.

Let's take the *fun* part first. It's fun to learn about colorful characters you can identify with who make lots of money while thumbing their noses at convention. In portraying these people Kennedy takes us on a rollicking, real-life romp through the bazaar we call our free enterprise system. You'll meet a motley parade of ingenious, independent, often outrageous capitalists strutting their stuff. They range from enterprising little guys who figure out ways to wangle entry-level jobs (though they don't stay there long) to the big-time entrepreneurs Kennedy knows personally who are making millions and billions. What helps make it all so enjoyable is that Kennedy's true-life characters have all beat the system, done it their way, and succeeded on their own terms. This is a gallery of self-made successes, people who often had to invent themselves from the bottom up.

Now let's look at why it's so *inspiring and motivating*. While going through this treasure trove of success stories, you're going to find yourself saying, time after time, "Hey, if they could do it, so can I!" And that's exactly the message I think we should be getting. Kennedy shows that our shortcomings are largely imaginary—excuses we dredge up to let ourselves off the hook. I recommend keeping several copies of this book around—which is exactly what I intend to do —so that you can treat yourself to a re-reading of how the heroes and heroines Kennedy writes about met and overcame challenges. Chances are you'll emulate them and figure out how to turn your perceived handicaps into advantages.

I am reminded of the long list of alibis that appears at the end of the classic self-help book *Think and Grow Rich*, by Napoleon Hill: *IF I had money . . . IF I had a good education . . . IF I had been given a chance . . . IF nothing happens to stop me . . . IF I had the talent that some people have . . . IF the boss only appreciated me . . . IF I only had time . . . IF I could just get started . . . IF I could meet the "right people." If* nothing, says Kennedy, noting that "if you want the odds on your side, you'll get off your butt and go to work turning your idea into a business." But let's say, for example, you don't have any capital; is that an excuse or a hard cold fact? Are the examples of entrepreneurs who started with no money applicable to us? As a matter of fact, starting off without resources—turning ideas into fortunes—is the essence of entrepreneurship. All the highly successful entrepreneurs I have met would rather have a great idea and no money than a million dollars and no ideas. After reading Kennedy's book you'll want to purge yourself of any such rationalizations you are nurturing and get on with the business of succeeding at something you enjoy. Fortunately, he gives us plenty of terrific examples, from eighth grade dropouts to housewives with no experience—people who started on the lowest rung—who had little else going for them but desire and guts. Whatever field you are in, these stories will excite your admiration and light a fire in your belly.

Finally, a few brief words about why this book is truly *profound*: I've been editing *Success* magazine for more than a decade and every example of self-made success that I have encountered is also a case study in breaking the rules. The way of the herd is not and cannot be the path to extraordinary accomplishment. If you simply do what the herd does, you'll end up where the herd is going. Notice that I say *every* example. I emphasize the point because I simply have not found any exceptions to this observation in my studies of exceptional entrepreneurs, achievers, and innovators. So, the ultimate lesson is that in order to attain entrepreneurial success you are not only *allowed* to break the rules, you are *required* to do so.

But does that mean you need to become a flamboyant renegade to be successful? Not at all—nor is that the real message of this book.

The rebels, heretics, and millionaire misfits that enliven these pages guarantee that reading this book will be an entertaining and unforgettable experience. But you'll also find that real power may consist of being different in your own quiet way. You may look like a conventional businessperson on the outside, but have a secret twist in your strategy that makes you more of an outrageous revolutionary than Dennis Rodman and Donald Trump combined. It's a matter of having the courage and insight to look at life and business from an independent perspective—and reading *No Rules* could be a major step in helping you gain that perspective.

The reason this book is so ideally suited to do just that can perhaps be best explained by a brief story about my previous career as the editor of a science magazine. In that job, I was always looking for examples of new breakthrough ideas and inventions. On the one hand, my editors and I tried to be open-minded about what we would take the time to look into, because we knew that almost every breakthrough, from the telephone to the airplane to laser surgery, was once considered "impossible" by the so-called experts. We also knew that some of the hottest inventions were created by "nobodies" working out of their garages. On the other hand, we knew that inventions could not violate the fundamental laws of science. We did not try to be so open-minded that our brains fell out. We did not abandon all standards of rationality and open the doors to every crank and crackpot with a perpetual motion machine.

In business terms, crank and crackpot ideas are often ones

that can't succeed because they ultimately produce no profits or satisfied customers. Some are simply misguided fantasies, while others are scams that make money for someone else at your expense. Some are "great ideas" but lousy business opportunities—for example, those with such low profit margins that they're not worth pursuing.

Fortunately, Kennedy is a hard-headed, street-smart, successful businessman who realizes that your real aim is to succeed or have a profitable business, and that breaking the rules is not an end in itself. He consistently sees beyond the standard wisdom to reveal the *real* business principles behind someone's success—for example, Edison's much-vaunted persistence in testing ten thousand different materials for the electric light bulb illuminates something different and more subtle than mere determination. There's also a vital principle of marketing in the story of Tom Monahan of Domino's Pizza—a principle that every successful business can apply.

In reading *No Rules*, you'll realize the world is a cornucopia of opportunities just off the beaten track and out of the mainstream—opportunities that in fact are often purposely suppressed by mainstream voices that don't want you to hear about them. I was fascinated by the accounts of people making money in activities ranging from investing in tax lien certificates to buying the beneficiary rights to insurance policies. Kennedy also helps you put the "get rich quick" stigma in perspective. As he points out, with some opportunities quick is the *only* way you'll get rich. So, if one of those ideas suits you, quit holding yourself back and go for it.

Yes, as Kennedy shows it's likely you are indeed holding yourself back—failing to see a wealth of opportunities—thanks to the long list of ill-advised rules and misleading "thou shalts" that bombard us all over the years.

Here's a chance to blow away those lies, myths, and fairy tales and get your life moving. It's a great opportunity. Seize it now.

Scott DeGarmo, formerly
Editor in Chief, *Success* magazine

AUTHOR'S INTRODUCTION

"Sometimes You Gotta Break the Rules"

"Not only have I broken all the rules I learned about—I have broken rules I didn't even know existed."

—Martin Scorsese

We are a people in search of rules.

It might have stopped when Moses came down from the mountain and announced: "Good news—I got Him down to ten." But even though few people manage to live by those, everybody wants more. Even the Catholics, who have lots of rules, still want more. In Washington, D.C., it takes a building to house all the rules already passed by all of the legislators who've trekked through there, yet today a session of Congress is still evaluated based on how many more rules it gets written and passed. In the arena of self-improvement and self-help, everybody creates rules. Napoleon Hill, in his classic best-seller *Think and Grow Rich*, had thirteen. In his contemporary best-seller *The 7 Habits of Highly Successful People*, Stephen Covey has seven. My speaking colleague Zig Ziglar has "10 Qualities of a Successful Person." In his speech on leadership, General Schwarzkopf even talks about "Rule #31" and "Rule #2."

So, how good are all these rules, anyway?

When You Meet the Buddha of Conventional Wisdom on the Road, Aim for Him and Push the Gas Pedal to the Floor

In the 1960s, every track and field coach taught every high jumper to run toward the bar and jump over it headfirst. Logic said this was right; obviously you want to look where you are going. And you want all the uninterrupted forward momentum you can get. But this kid, Dick Fosbury, began fooling around with a twist, a turn, and going over the high bar backwards. As he approached the bar, he planted his right foot, spun a full 180 degrees, and launched himself backwards over the bar. *Time* magazine then called it "the most preposterous high jumping technique ever devised." Of course, everybody laughed. His move was called "the Fosbury Flop." There was some question as to its legality in competition. But to every expert's chagrin, Dick not only stuck with it but won in the Olympics doing the Fosbury Flop.

This is not the only time that "conventional wisdom" has been embarrassed.

The Ultimate Cliché: "Rules Are Made to Be Broken"

This is a book about cliché-busting. Yet it turns out that the ultimate cliché—rules are made to be broken—may be the most valid of all.

The story of the Fosbury Flop takes me back. As a kid, on the backyard court, I played basketball, and I threw my foul shots in one-handed, like throwing a baseball. I made just about every foul shot. It took a junior high school gym teacher weeks to drill that out of me and force me to use the "correct" two-handed, body-square-to-the-backboard foul-shooting position. Doing it "correctly," I missed about two-thirds of the shots. Still do. (And he just cut the heart right out of me about that game. Were it not for him and his stupid rule, I might have gone on to play, a college scholarship, and wound up being like Dennis Rodman.)

I've always doubted all conventional wisdom. In fact, I was asked to leave catechism classes at our family's Lutheran church, never to return, because I was asking too many questions. I don't remember the guy's name, but the minister who taught those classes had really baggy pants, and I usually got him so mad with my questions he would go into a tirade, face glowing red, actually feverishly jumping up and down for several minutes. I measured my effectiveness by how far up his legs his baggy pants went.

That Kid Who Won't Stop Asking Questions Grows Up

My main business is advertising. And there are a zillion rules about how to create good advertising. There is a wealth of conventional wisdom. I have made an entire career out of violating all this wisdom, all these rules.

In the January 1993 issue of a trade magazine for the nonprofit field, *Fund Raising Management*, an article by industry expert Mal Warwick ran, with this title: "The 11 Cardinal Rules of Copywriting—and How to Break Them." You do not need to read this article to get value from it. The headline alone says a lot. It reminds us that in EVERY field, there are rules for successful achievement—that *are* made to be broken. Let me give you a great example from the direct response advertising field. For maybe thirty years, the "rule" for a full-page, copy-intensive direct response ad was to put a coupon in the lower right-hand corner, and to make that coupon very clearly stand out, even jump out of the rest of the ad. Typically using a big, thick dotted-line border, a bold headline like "Free Trial Coupon" or "Order Form." Even as the toll-free 800 number and credit card ordering by phone came onto the scene, this "rule" remained and was adhered to. Until a few people, like me, Mark Haroldsen, and a couple other advertisers broke the rule. Today about a third of all such ads use the "new couponless format" we pioneered, where there is no coupon; instead, the ordering instructions are written into the copy, in a seamless flow, and the customer is asked to call an 800 number OR take a plain piece of paper and write his name, address, and other information on it and fax it in or mail it in to a provided address. But there's no coupon to fill out and tear out. In many cases, this proves to increase response—presumably because it increases readership; the absence of the coupon lets the ad look more like an article. In the late 1980s, however, I began experimenting, very successfully, with a now much copied violation of this format: couponless ordering instructions combined with a lengthier summary of the offer in a box with a border around it. This approach not only violates the rules, it defies logic. It reveals at a glance that the ad is an ad, not an article, and while it does not provide the convenience of a coupon, it boosts response. How can that be? Got me. But sometimes it pays to break the rules just to break the rules.

This Book Even Argues with Itself

Maybe the best part of this book is that it can't even agree with itself.

My friend, Herb True, a management professor at Notre Dame, tells me that a lot of kids go into shock when he gives them several books to read, each one presenting a conflicting viewpoint on the same issue. They come back and want him to tell them which of the authors is "right."

On one level, I'd like things to be that simple. Just give me *one* set of instructions. On the other hand, not only am I sure that nobody has the one fits-all, solves-all, handles-every-situation set of instructions, I'm also sure if somebody did have it, they'd disagree with it half the time. The only folks I'd ever met who are absolutely dead-on certain that they know the right thing to do in every circumstance, for themselves and everybody else around them, are just like that Jim Jones guy who wound up leading his followers to mass suicide in Guyana. Anybody that certain of his rules is dangerous.

Still, even as we see that rules don't always work, we go looking for more rules.

Nowhere Are There More Rules Than in How-to-Succeed Land

Beginning in 1975, I officially joined the "success education industry," populated by thousands of speakers, seminar leaders, authors, gurus, psychologists, and organizations, from the very staid Dale Carnegie folks to, well, remember EST? In recent years, about a third of my life has been as a professional speaker, addressing over two hundred thousand people a year and appearing at many events with big-name "success speakers" like Zig Ziglar, Jim Rohn, and Tom Hopkins. One of my best clients, the Guthy-Renker Corporation, produces the Tony Robbins infomercials. Millions of dollars of my own how-to-succeed books, cassettes, and other products have been sold. And, in this book, I chew vigorously on that hand that has fed me and feeds me so well.

Among the classic ideas and axioms about success in business and success in life that we turn inside out and look at with a jaundiced eye here, together, many are the "treasures" of the "success industry." Some of my colleagues may very well hate this book. And that's okay with me. I figure: If you don't offend somebody at least once a day, you're not saying much. The opportunity to offend tens of thousands with a book like this was irresistible.

Oh, and about those Catholics. I was raised a Lutheran, which is a Catholic but without confession, the little glasses of wine and the cookies, or our own infomercials at Easter and Christmas. When I was a kid, we had good friends who owned a little neighborhood restaurant and take-out joint in Parma, Ohio, right smack in the middle of a Catholic parish, near a very big church. This place's owners made their living off the Friday fish dinner business. From 4:00 to 7:00 P.M., an ocean of fried fish in Styrofoam containers went out their door. Enough tartar sauce in little paper cups to drown Moby Dick. We even ate fish every Friday—religiously—and we weren't Catholic. As I understood the deal, if you ate meat on Friday, you guaranteed yourself a seat in hell for all eternity, and we weren't taking any chances. I wonder what somebody thinks who hates fish but eats it every Friday, 52 Fridays a year, for, say, twenty years, 1,040 Fridays, in order to stay out of hell, then gets the word: Hey, we changed the rules. It's okay now to eat anything you want on Friday. Huh? What happened here? Is hell full? Did they catch the pope wolfing down a couple Big Macs on a Friday? Did word come down from the sky: "I'm sick of eating fish every Friday!" What?

You could be following some rule just like that, which some years down the road, some authority's going to change, just like that fish-on-Fridays deal. Let's find out.

Forget Just About Everything You Were Ever Told About Positive Thinking and Motivation

"Thought is subversive and revolutionary, destructive and terrible, thought is merciless to privilege, established institutions and comfortable habit. Thought looks into the pit of hell and is not afraid. Thought is great and swift and free, the light of the world, and the chief glory of man."
—Bertrand Russell, mathematician, philosopher, Nobel laureate

In the 1995 Kentucky Derby, famous trainer D. Wayne Lukas sent a horse named Prince of Thieves and another horse named Grindstone to the gate, both with famous, top jockeys: Pat Day on Prince of Thieves, Jerry Bailey on Grindstone. Prince of Thieves was picked by many to win. Grindstone was picked by no one. Prince never got in gear. Grindstone came from way behind, in a thrilling stretch drive, to "steal" the race. Grindstone, however, injured himself in his herculean effort and was promptly retired to stud, not to go on to the second race in the Triple Crown. Incredibly, Lukas then yanked Day from Prince of Thieves and replaced him with Bailey for the Preakness. This was a huge slap in the face to the all-star jockey who had won four previous Preaknesses, including two for Lukas. It'd be akin to benching a quarterback like Troy Aikman or Steve Young after one disappointing game. It was the talk of the racing world. And it set up one of the great moments of sports.

Two weeks later, at Pimlico in Baltimore, Jerry Bailey rode D. Wayne Lukas's highly touted Prince of Thieves in the Preakness Stakes. As always, Lukas was much interviewed before the race, and very visible in the stands as post time approached. The deposed Pat Day picked up a mount from another trainer, and he went to the gate on Louis Quatorze, a ten-to-one long shot that had finished a dismal sixteenth in the Derby. When the gate opened, Quatorze buckled, but Day steadied him, straightened him out, and took the lead—and never looked back. Day rode Louis Quatorze to a blistering $1:53\frac{1}{2}$ for the one and three-sixteenths mile race, matching the record for the race set twelve years before.

As he sailed across the finish line, standing in the stirrups, he looked in the direction of Mr. Lukas, then to the TV cameras, and defiantly waved his hand, wiggling all five fingers and shouting "Five."

"Five!"

It was one of those magic moments when somebody who has been underestimated or ridiculed gets to triumph. Every Thoroughbred jockey and even every Standardbred driver in America was rooting for Pat Day and reveled in the "Up yours, Lukas!" emotion that surged through him as he pushed that second-rate horse to a record-setting Preakness victory.

Pat Day rode the race of his life, motivated not by any pure, elegant, charitable, or noble impulses. He rode the race of his life motivated by—*revenge!*

Anybody who has ever been "crapped on" can identify with Pat Day. I watched it too. I bet on Louis Quartoze only because I wanted Day to stick it to Lukas. I was in a hotel room an hour or so after giving a speech, on the edge of my seat on a footstool in front of the TV, urging him on and yelling "Yes!" as he gave his salute to Lukas.

I was reminded of a speech I heard twenty years ago or so. I was in an audience at a huge Amway "rally." The speaker was a fellow by the name of Charlie Marsh, an ex-cop, ex–bus driver, ex–milk truck driver, oft-fired, failed in business ventures, sneered upon and laughed at by all his friends and relatives when he started in the Amway business. Charlie told of inviting his friends to his first "living room meeting" and standing there at the door at 7:00, 7:30, 8:00, 8:30, finally realizing that no one was coming, then retreating to the bathroom to hide from the critical eyes of his wife. Of standing in the bathroom, looking in the mirror, and seeing a loser. Of getting mad at himself and everyone he knew.

Presumably to the amazement of everyone he knew, Charlie went on to become a Crown Direct Distributor in the Amway system, worth at least $250,000 a year in income and probably more.

In that same speech, he told of being driven by his anger and disappointment and resentment over the way his friends treated him that night. He told of inviting all his relatives, neighbors, and everybody he knew down to the dock for the bon voyage party as he and his wife, Elsie, departed on their first award-winners' cruise. He told of standing on the deck of the ship, confetti flying, glass of champagne in hand, looking down at the cluster of people on the dock who had ridiculed him and—triumphantly giving them the finger!

Most successful people choose not to talk about it, but many were and are motivated by very ignoble, "negative" emotions. I don't think any author of any of the gazillion how-to-succeed books has ever addressed this. Instead, most preach the idea that you must eradicate, suppress, or give up all such negative emotions, forgive everybody, and focus only on positive, happy thoughts. And that sounds right. But reality does not prove it to be true.

And this is just one of a number of ways that "positive thinking" is misunderstood and misused.

With Apologies to Dr. Norman Vincent Peale, Here's What's Wrong with Positive Thinking

My mother was a huge fan of Norman Vincent Peale and you may be too. I met the late Dr. Peale on two occasions, and have since spoken at events where Mrs. Peale has appeared. I like them both, I certainly respect his enormous influence, and I am convinced he may be one of the most misinterpreted, misunderstood authors in our genre. Were he alive, I think he'd applaud *this* book.

Here are the main ways people get misled with "positive thinking."

#1: "Don't Be Negative!"

This is the cry of the demented organization turning against its sole, sane voice. I have many times observed the individual who dares to raise questions about the viability of a particular idea shouted down with "Don't be negative."

There is a joke many motivational speakers tell, as a positive illustration of positive thinking: A guy has tripped and fallen off the roof of a thirty-story building. He is falling toward certain death. Someone yells out the fifteenth-story window, "How are you doing?" And the falling fellow hollers back, "Okay so far!" This has been told at countless sales meetings and seminars. But it is NOT an accurate representation of "positive thinking" as Peale meant it to be. It does not illustrate positive thinking. It illustrates stupidity.

The idea that raising questions, doubt, skepticism, reasons why something may not work, marks you as a "negative thinker," a cancer to be cut out, a dangerous voice to be ignored is sick and stupid.

Cynicism *is* unhealthy. Optimism *is* helpful and desirable. But blind, stubborn, unwarranted optimism is *stupid*.

If you happen to be a sales manager reading this, I have some specific, contrarian advice for you. Instead of going into the weekly meeting as a low-rent motivational blowhard, exhorting the troops to "think positive" and decrying those who dare "think negative," dig in and do a real job, so you can go in there with a prospecting, marketing, and sales plan of substance so that the troops have something worth being optimistic about.

And, for salespeople, negotiators, or others who seek to persuade or influence, I teach "the positive power of negative preparation": carefully identifying and acknowledging every possible objection that may be raised, every reason for saying no or stalling possible, and every flaw or weakness in your product, service, or proposition. Get all that "negative stuff" down on paper. Then you can intelligently prepare to deal with those things. Then you will not be "thrown for a loop" when these things raise their ugly heads. Then you can reasonably and realistically expect positive outcomes.

Mike Vance, a long-time, close associate of Walt Disney, today a popular lecturer on creativity, once said you could distill Dale Carnegie's advice to "smile whether you feel like it or not," but that a much better idea was "get a reason to smile so you can feel like it."

#2: Positive Thinking as Panacea

Having carefully read every one of Dr. Peale's books and talked with him personally at some length, I can assure you that he never meant for people to go sit in the corner, think positive thoughts, and expect riches to materialize in the backyard. Yet a lot of people sally forth believing that if they just think positive thoughts, everything in their life is supposed to change as a result. There are even a few metaphysical-leaning motivational speakers who teach such silliness.

I remember getting my first brand-new car. I had owned and driven a sequence of really pitiful junkers, out of necessity. In fact, I bought my first car for $25, my second for $300. In both cases, I got my money's worth, so you can imagine what I was driving around in. Well, when I got my first brand-new car, it was a great disappointment to discover that the birds crapped on it with impunity. That seemed unfair. If I were setting up the system, I'd restrict the birds to crapping only on old, cheap, ugly cars. But birds crap democratically and indiscriminately. They're not alone in that trait.

You can think positive all you want and you are still going to spill coffee on your new tie, get a flat tire, get cut off on the freeway, lose a big sale, get cheated, and be disappointed from time to time. Positive thinking is not about eliminating all of that from life. It is a tool to be used in more effectively coping with such events.

People who believe you can prevent problems with positive thoughts like some magic amulet hung around the neck wind up cynical, negative thinkers. People who use positive thinking like kids use whistling in the dark to keep bogeymen away are doomed to disappointment and depression. People who insist on walking around with eyes closed to "the negative" are just as likely to walk in front of an oncoming train as they are to fall into a bed of roses.

#3: Only Noble, Positive Emotions Contribute to Success

This brings us back to the Pat Day and Charlie Marsh stories.

Last season, we watched the aging running back Marcus Allen muster up a phenomenal game for the Kansas City Chiefs, thus taking the Raiders out of the play-offs. Allen was motivated by his hatred for the Raiders' owner Al Davis, who had stuck Allen on the Raiders bench for two years and virtually killed Allen's career. When the name "Al Davis" is mentioned, bile crawls quickly up Marcus Allen's throat. Does Marcus Allen take his performance up a few notches every time he plays against the Raiders? You bet he does.

The late Dean Martin, never known for his work ethic, admitted that he knuckled down and worked harder in the years immediately following his breakup with Jerry Lewis than at any time before or after that in his career, because he was angered by both critics' and friends' dire predictions of his career's demise; that everybody thought Lewis was the talent carrying Martin. Late in Dean's life, an interviewer ticked off some of his notable accomplishments, including a gold record that unseated the Beatles from the top of the charts, a diverse movie career, and a long-running television show. "Guess I showed Jerry," he said. It was a revealing comment.

I frequently meet incredibly successful people in different fields who confess, sometimes publicly but mostly privately, to being highly motivated by a desire to "show 'em."

I also know people motivated by fear and paranoia. One businessman I know, who rose up out of a very embarrassing, much publicized bankruptcy to build a $20 million-a-year company, told me he gets up every morning and works hard all day, constantly looking for developing problems to nip in the bud, and goes to bed every night worrying about what he may have missed, because he fears that it is all going to end tomorrow.

"What will I do," he asked me, "if people suddenly stop answering my ads?"

Who is to say what should motivate you? Whatever works.

There's no doubt that emotional forces like anger, resentment, desire for revenge, or fear of failure can have very unpleasant side effects, ranging from the destruction of personal relationships to ill health. But not to acknowledge that a great deal of positive accomplishment is birthed by such emotions is Pollyannaish. The real motivations behind many success stories are a far cry from happy-face, positive, noble emotions, and that's a fact.

But Here's the Biggest Flaw of All with Positive Thinking

In 1960, a plastic surgeon turned amateur psychologist, Dr. Maxwell Maltz, wrote and had published a book that would take off, achieve blockbuster best-seller status, and revolutionize the entire field of self-improvement. His book, *Psycho-Cybernetics*, went on to reach over thirty million people, and lives on today, long after his death. These days, you can still buy the book, on the shelf after thirty years, in bookstores, buy audiocassettes based on the book in bookstores, and get complete home study courses, seminars, a newsletter, and more from The Psycho-Cybernetics Foundation.* I know, because I'm a founding board member of the Foundation and a zealous advocate of the "Zero Resistance Living System" birthed from Dr. Maltz's works.

Dr. Maltz came forward with the reason why so many people earnestly attempt to improve their lives with positive thinking but never get anywhere. At the time, his was a radical and controversial concept. Today, just about every book, tape, seminar, philosophy, or approach for helping people help themselves includes Dr. Maltz's discoveries.

In brief, Dr. Maltz became convinced that no amount of conscious positive thinking or attempts at willpower and self-

*For a FREE audiocassette about Psycho-Cybernetics and Zero Resistance Living, fax a request to The Psycho-Cybernetics Foundation at 602/269-3113.

discipline can overcome a negative self-image. Another way to say this is that whenever resolution is incongruent with the self-image, the resolution fails. This explains sincere, earnest dieters who cannot stick to a weight loss regimen, why New Year's resolutions are never kept, why people procrastinate, and much more.

It is the self-image that governs what a person "can" and "can't" do. So, for example, if deep down inside the self-image, a person sees himself as "athletically impaired," clumsy, the last kid to ever get picked to play a game, he can take golf lessons, watch golf videos, use golf gadgets, and learn the technical aspects of a good golf swing, but his actual game will "snap back" to conform to the embedded, governing images. Maltz was adamant that consciously set goals and consciously held thoughts have little power and no chance of lasting impact if they are not congruent with the images and beliefs embedded in the subconscious, and he went on to develop unique "mental training exercises" to identify what is in your self-image and to modify it as you choose. These "mental training exercises" have been used and endorsed by countless famous Olympic and pro athletes, authors, entertainment personalities, business leaders, and others.

My own experience with Psycho-Cybernetics begins in my teen years, where Maltz's discoveries and methods helped me conquer a severe stuttering problem when all other attempts to resolve it had failed. This stuttering kid has become one of the highest paid professional business speakers in America today.

It so happens that Dr. Peale and Dr. Maltz became friends, and Norman Vincent Peale frequently acknowledged the importance of Maltz's writings and work.

Why "Getting Motivated" Is All Too Often an Illusion

I tell a true story about the life insurance industry. In Akron, Ohio, where I grew up, a bunch of insurance companies all have their offices lined up on Market Street, very near to a little shopping center in which there is a popular breakfast joint called The Egg Castle. Every morning, the insurance reps gather in their morning meetings and repeat positive affirmations, sing the company songs, march around the table, listen to motivational tapes, watch motivational videos, and get pumped up. Then, ten feet tall and bulletproof, they make a last stop at The Egg Castle for a last injection of caffeine. If you want to see "motivation," be there at The Egg Castle at 10:00 A.M.—but be careful not to get trampled as all the super-motivated salespeople rush out to conquer the world. If you listen, you'll hear things like "Today's my million dollar day" . . . "I'm gonna hit it right out of the park today."

Now here's what's fascinating. In that same shopping center, there was a restaurant and tavern called The Dry Dock. There, happy hour started every day at 4:00 P.M. For you tee-totalers, "happy hour" (sometimes called "attitude adjustment hour") involves two drinks for the price of one and free food. Anyplace there are two drinks for the price of one and free food, you'll find plenty of insurance salespeople. So, at 4:00 P.M.—whoosh!—all these reps return to the roost. But they are changed men and women. Gone is all the "motivation." Now they shuffle their feet, slump their shoulders, look at the ground, and say things like "Can't sell life insurance in this town. Everybody's getting laid off," "I never get the good leads," . . . and so on.

So here's the $64,000 question: Where'd all that super-charged "motivation" go?

It was an illusion in the first place.

It was what I call "motivation without foundation," which can only lead to frustration, ultimately cynicism.

This is why, incidentally, I refuse any speaking engagement where I am prohibited from selling from the platform my "tool kits." To get people all jazzed up about my ideas and then send them home without the tools they need to make real changes and without securing their commitment to doing so is just one giant waste of everybody's time. By noon the next day, the nice warm feeling has worn off. It's over.

The truth is that JUST "getting motivated" is futile, just as is "thinking positive."

CONTRARIAN SUCCESS STRATEGY:

Give up forced "positive thinking" or "motivation"; instead build a solid foundation of a strong self-image, well-defined goals, practical plans, and know-how that naturally produce positive expectancy, initiative, and follow-through.

The Myth of the Born Salesman.
Or Born Anything.

*Kid to his father, about a report card filled with Fs: "Well, Dad,
what do you think the problem is: heredity or environment?"*

Is there such a thing as a "born" anything?

Is there such a thing as a "born salesman"? Or someone born NEVER to be a salesman. If you look at the birth announcements in the newspaper, you will see that there are lots of little baby boys and little baby girls born, but you won't find any birth announcements of little baby salesmen or saleswomen. My speaking colleague Zig Ziglar claims that when he was born in Yazoo City, Mississippi, it was written up as the birth of a salesman. I doubt it. And the truth behind the career of Zig, maybe, arguably one of the greatest and most famous salesmen of all time, is that he was a dismal failure, a complete incompetent early on.

Many people tremendously limit themselves and their options by stubbornly believing that successful people in different fields were "born" to do what they do, "naturals" at what they do.

There ARE, of course, certain people the camera loves, who become successful models, actresses, or actors. On the other hand, the legendary singer Tony Bennett (whom I talk about

later in this book for a different reason) is one of many entertainers who suffered from and had to overcome great stage
fright. But there are apparently entertainers virtually born to
entertain. There are people with great innate athletic talent
who become Michael Jordan or Emmitt Smith. But even these
"naturals" are deceptive in two ways: First, they are few. Rare.
Aberrant. Second, even they must work very hard and do work
very hard to capitalize on their innate talents.

Most successful people are definitely NOT born to do what
they wind up doing so well that it looks easy and natural to
others. Here are some examples:

Go back to selling for a minute and consider Joe Girard, several times recognized in *The Guiness Book of World Records* as
"The World's Greatest Salesman." At age forty-nine, Joe had
been the number one automobile salesman for eleven consecutive years. Here *must* be a "born salesman." But Joe was thrown
out of high school, lasted only ninety-seven days in the army,
was fired from forty different jobs, and even failed as a thief. Joe
says, "People tell me that I'm a born salesman. Let me tell you
that's not true. I made me a salesman, all by myself. And if I
could do it, starting from where I did, anybody can." Joe and I
also share a bit of background; we both struggled with stuttering early in life. Imagine a stuttering salesman—or a stuttering public speaker!

How about Richard Branson, the man behind Virgin Airways?
As of this writing, he is arguably one of the world's most successful, famous, and often outrageous entrepreneurs. He has
taken on giant British Airways and confounded them, pro-
moted the Sex Pistols, launched his own brands of vodka and
condoms—and virtually every business he has touched in
twenty-five years has turned gold. As the leader of a multimillion-dollar conglomerate, Branson is about as contrarian as
you can get. He runs the enterprises from an office in his
home, can't operate a computer, relies totally on pen and pad,
and frequently jumps into businesses he knows nothing about.
Most interesting is how much he has been in the public eye
since age nineteen and how he has driven many of his businesses to success largely on the strength of flamboyant personal promotion and publicity, yet he is shy and often very

inarticulate. He is a high school dropout with no educational preparation for anything he has done. Despite the decades of experience he has had with the media—with interviews, TV appearances, giving speeches—he remains obviously uncomfortable with the entire process of communication. A biographer of Branson, Tim Jackson, author of *Virgin King: Inside Richard Branson's Business Empire*, traces this nagging insecurity and discomfort back to Branson's poor performance in school and incomplete education. It is impossible to judge Branson as someone for whom success is "natural." In many ways, Richard Branson became a billionaire in spite of himself.

"The Natural": As Rare as the Unicorn. As Hard to Spot as the Loch Ness Monster.

If you have been told and now believe that you have no natural talent for something you really want to do, you may be best advised to go ahead and do it anyway. After all, how do you KNOW what talent you have until you REALLY test it? Comedian Red Skelton, singers Tony Bennett and Frank Sinatra, have all proven to be very "talented" artists. Their careers with paintbrush in hand have been every bit as distinguished and celebrated as their first careers. Fran Tarkenton made the transition from "jock" to super-entrepreneur. Joan Rivers made the transition from entertainer to entrepreneur AND jewelry designer. Darren Bennett of the NFL San Diego Chargers is an Australian soccer player who decided to try out as a field goal kicker while here in the United States on vacation. Best-selling novelist Scott Turow: an attorney. My former client, now business partner, Jeff Paul was a Certified Financial Planner who has discovered and developed such a "talent" for direct response advertising and mail-order copywriting that he rivals the best known, highest paid pros in that field, has made millions of dollars doing so, and has had one of his penned sales letters reprinted in the book *The 100 Greatest Sales Letters Ever Written*. Debbi Fields had no known business acumen or experience when she started Mrs. Fields' Cookies from scratch, yet it quickly became apparent that she had tremendous entrepreneurial "talents." More recently, she has tested herself and proven to be a "talented," dynamic, effective professional speaker. I could fill the book with such examples.

Your past—your past beliefs about your talents and abilities, your past experiences with your talents and abilities or lack thereof, what you've been told in the past about your talents and abilities—need only define your future if you let it. You either give or deny permission to your past to control your future.

Forget All About Aptitude Tests

My aptitude tests in high school—remember those?—suggested I'd make a good social worker or a concert pianist. I happen to be devoid of any sense of rhythm or appreciation for classical music and, philosophically, politically, I'm a bit to the right of Rush Limbaugh. So much for aptitude tests. In fact, the activities in which I have become very successful and from which I make large sums of money are instructive because of how ill suited by "natural ability" I am to them. For example, for nearly twenty years, I have made hundreds of thousands of dollars a year as a professional speaker. I stuttered badly for a while in youth, I was shy (I still, frankly, am not much of a "people person"), and when I started speaking I was downright awful, awkward, and uncomfortable. My earliest audiocassettes are so bad and embarrassing I try to buy them back when I find them. I make the lion's share of my living writing; six books have gone through bookstores, well over a million dollars a year of my self-published books, manuals, and courses are sold worldwide, and thousands of people part with $199 a year to get my newsletter. As I recall I got a C in creative writing, a B in journalism, and my English teacher in my junior and senior years in high school suggested I'd make a great plumber. Several critics have made similar suggestions since then. And I would agree only to this extent: I doubt very seriously that I have any "natural" writing talent. But I certainly can write for dough.

I think the idea of "natural ability" is, at best, irrelevant. The argument of genetics versus education and environment is almost irrelevant. Not necessarily invalid, just irrelevant. If you are limited in a particular area, if you really do lack natural talent, you can make up for it if you determine to do so. If you happen to have some natural talent in an area in which you desire to excel, celebrate and build on the advantage gratefully. But either way, you can do pretty much whatever you set your mind to do.

On the other hand, everybody has and ought to find certain things they do better than others. Not everybody ought to be an entrepreneur, for example. Some people think they are entrepreneurs because they have proven to be unemployable. But that doesn't qualify you as an entrepreneur. A refugee maybe. But not an entrepreneur. To be a successful entrepreneur, you need to have or develop great vision, ambition, thick skin, immunity to discouragement, and ability to live with isolation. These are not characteristics everybody would *want* to have. And just because you got cut loose from your middle management position in a corporate downsizing and you can spell "consultant" doesn't mean you ought to be one. In fact, I'm astounded at the number of people who jump into different businesses with little thought about whether or not they will like them and are eager to develop the skills and characteristics most likely to contribute to success in that endeavor. People will ask me: What are the "hot" opportunities? What's a good business to get into? But the smart question is: What's the best business *for me* to get into? Very different answers for different people.

Not because you can't. You *can* do just about anything.

Because you shouldn't. Based on who you are AND who you are eager to become. In fact, some excellent career or business advice is to pick endeavors because of the type of person the endeavors will force you to become! An early mentor used to urge people of very limited financial means to commit to the goal of becoming a millionaire, not so much for the money, he explained, but because of the people they would have to become, the positive characteristics and behaviors they would have to develop in order to achieve the financial benchmark.

He was widely misunderstood on this point and perceived by some to be a preacher of greed. What he meant, simply was: Big commitment to big goals builds big people.

Forget All About IQ Tests

For years, educators, parents, and everybody else devoutly believed in the predictive value of IQ tests. Today, psychologists agree that IQ measures only about 20 percent of the factors that determine success, so that high IQ versus low IQ cannot reliably forecast who will be successful or unsuccessful in life in general or in any given career or business field. Eighty percent of all that determines success comes from factors that are not measured by IQ. This led to the very successful 1995 book *Emotional Intelligence* by Daniel Goldman, Ph.D., a former Harvard lecturer and *New York Times* reporter on behavioral and brain sciences. Goldman has found the traditional measurements of intelligence unsatisfactory in predicting how people live their lives. Why doesn't the smartest kid in class automatically wind up the richest? The happiest? Why are some people buoyant when awash in adversity while others crumble? With "EQ," Goldman has attempted to define a new and different standard, a more accurate measurement of a person's reactions to life situations.

Incidentally, while it may be quite difficult to raise or improve IQ in adulthood, it is certainly possible and comparatively easy or at least formulaic to deliberately modify and alter EQ at virtually any age.

In the book *Profiles of Power and Success: Fourteen Geniuses Who Broke The Rules*, author Gene Landrum concludes that "too much money or education or IQ is actually counterproductive to achievement." How can that be? The "psychobiographies" of the world's greatest innovators and entrepreneurs this author studied conclusively prove that intelligence is way down the list of important criteria for high achievement or attaining power in virtually any profession. A former president of Harvard is quoted as saying, "Test scores have a modest correlation with first-year grades and no correlation with what you do in the rest of your life." It appears possible to be, in street language, too smart for your own good. Such people are often excessively analytical and immobilized by all the factors that go into making decisions; unable to communicate their ideas to the masses in a manner that is easily understood and accepted; and otherwise impaired when it comes to simply getting things done.

I used to have a mentor who accused high-IQers of being so smart they could spell "horse" in seven languages but so dumb they'd buy a cow to ride. It seems that "common sense," "street smarts," or "practical know-how" may overcome innate super-intelligence more often than not.

CONTRARIAN SUCCESS STRATEGY:

Stop worrying about genetics, so-called natural talent, or what others have said or say about your IQ, your talent, your ability, your aptitude. You may or may not have handicaps or weaknesses, but if you do, it is your choice whether they serve as barriers that restrict you or as hurdles that challenge you to rise above them and leap over them. Not IQ, not birth order, not astrology, not others' evaluations of you—nothing has as much power to determine what you will do and how well you will do it as your own decisions and determination.

CHAPTER 3

"You Can't Get Anywhere These Days Without a College Education."

"When I was in junior high school, the teachers voted me the student most likely to end up in the electric chair."
—Sylvester Stallone

Fifteen years ago, college-educated folks earned about 40 percent more than high school grads. Today, it's about a 60 percent plus. That IS an argument in favor of a college education. But look closer and here is what you will discover: If college actually prepares you for anything, it is for a job. To earn 60 percent more than the lesser educated do in jobs. College does not prepare you to be entrepreneurial, and it certainly does not prepare you to get rich.

An old mentor of mine used to include in his speeches his story of graduating from high school in Boaz, Alabama, and being eager to get into the University of Alabama, where Bear Bryant coached, until he called up, asked for their course in becoming a millionaire, and discovered they didn't have one. Then he called around to a dozen other universities and, to his utter amazement, found that they didn't offer such a course either. That ended his interest in attending college.

The list of supersuccessful people who dropped out of high school or college or who never went to college is lengthy.

I got to spend a little bit of time with Tom Monaghan when working on Guthy-Renker's TV infomercial for "Think and Grow Rich," and that inspired me to thoroughly research Tom's life and experiences. I use a Tom Monaghan "marketing secret" in just about every one of my speeches and seminars. When Tom opened the little pizza joint that was the beginning of Domino's, he was twenty-three years old, with no college degree, virtually no business experience, no mentors, and no money. The early days were very unencouraging. First week's sales: $99. But twenty-five years later, the Domino's empire included over 2,500 outlets spanning all fifty states and six foreign countries. By 1986, it was a $2 billion-a-year enterprise.

Tom did a brilliant thing. My friend Al Ries, coauthor of the famous book on advertising, *Positioning: The Battle for Your Mind*, says: If you can't be first in a category, set up a new category that you can be first in. Tom Monaghan did that by creating a pizza DELIVERY system. Then he based his powerful Unique Selling Proposition on that: "Fresh, hot pizza delivered in 30 minutes or less, guaranteed." Pretty smart stuff for a guy with no degree. Don't you need a degree in marketing from the Harvard Business School to come up with such brilliant stuff? Apparently not.

Also in fast food, Dave Thomas, founder of Wendy's, left school after the tenth grade. He just earned his high school equivalency diploma in 1993. But he got his practical, achievement-oriented education by beginning work at a lunch counter at age twelve, a brief stint as a cook in the army, work in several restaurants, a "break" as manager of a failing Kentucky Fried Chicken. His own business has grown from the first Wendy's, in 1969, to over four thousand units. Dave learned everything he knows about picking locations, hiring, managing, advertising, and finance on the run. "I know how to make a great hamburger," he says, "that's *my* experience." And he believes that marketers often "outthink" themselves. "There are a lot of guys in nice offices who get involved in complicated theories, but people want what they've always wanted. Quality. Their money's worth," Dave says. "I've kept this business as simple as possible. We give customers good food. We have clean restaurants, staffed by clean, polite people. And we offer the food at a good price. *That's* our marketing strategy."

Brad Daniel dropped out of the University of Florida to focus on his then part-time, fledgling business. He told *Success* magazine: "School didn't stimulate me. It was frustrating being taught by professors who have never been in the real business world." At age twenty-six, Brad oversees a growing franchise network of forty Balloons&Bears flower, gift basket, and teddy bear stores, in 1995 generating $4.5 million in sales.

Every year, while growing up, he saw and made notes on over two hundred movies and by sixth grade he was writing film scripts. But his grades were terrible, school bored him to tears, so Quentin Tarantino dropped out of high school. As a teen, lying about his age, he started his career as an usher in a porno theater. "To me, it was the most ironic situation: I finally got a job at a movie theater and it's a place where I don't want to watch the movies!" Thanks to his encyclopedic knowledge of the movies, he got a job at a large video store and quickly became its manager. While holding down that job, he got bit acting parts, wrote, sold, and lost control of a script subsequently made into a movie that failed at the box office. His first big break came when an established producer raised financing for Tarantino's script for the movie *Reservoir Dogs*, thanks largely to actor Harvey Keitel's enthusiasm for the script. Now we all know Quentin Tarantino very well as a result of his 1994 blockbuster success, the movie *Pulp Fiction*, credited, incidentally, with the rebirth of John Travolta's career. Tarantino is a pure contrarian. He has ignored conventional industry wisdom at virtually every opportunity. His films are violent to the point of controversy, at a time when Hollywood is under political and public pressure to rein in movie screen violence. His movies are thoughtful to the point of dispensing philosophy. He will be a force in the movie industry for many years to come.

A favorite story of mine is Dunkin' Donuts. In 1950, in Quincy, Massachusetts, a high school dropout, Bill Rosenberg, created Dunkin' Donuts. Over a thirty-year span, this dropout built a company with two thousand stores in fourteen countries and made millions for his family and many of his franchisees.

Today, his son is in charge of the ever-expanding, billion-dollar-a-year empire. Robert Rosenberg took the reins at age twenty-six, immediately after Harvard Graduate School of Business. But you should not be fooled by the Harvard credential. Robert learned Dunkin' Donuts inside out by working a different job every summer since age fifteen. At age fifty-seven, "Junior" must now wrestle with the gourmet coffeehouse competition—notably Starbucks, the health-conscious consumer's aversion to fatty, high-calorie doughnuts, and the need to keep a mature company growing. His Harvard lessons will undoubtedly come in handy. But this is an empire founded and built on "common sense," and that will still be most important.

Kirk Kerkorian made millions during his career buying and selling Las Vegas hotels and properties, making deals in Hollywood, and frugally investing. Today he is one of the biggest shareholders in Chrysler. He is a junior high school dropout.

Wayne Huizenga, who I talk about at some length elsewhere in this book, dropped out of college and started a trash-hauling business with an old, decrepit pickup truck. By age thirty-one, his Waste Management, Inc., was the largest waste services company in the world. You know Huizenga these days for his Blockbuster Video empire and his sports interests.

Helena Rubinstein is one of the biggest names in the beauty business. She dropped out of a tech school after struggling as a very poor student.

Then there's me. In idle, casual, rapport-building conversation over coffee or lunch, clients frequently ask me where I went to school. Sometimes their disappointment at hearing "Revere High School, Richfield, Ohio," is written all over their faces. Some even press it: "How did you learn to do what you do?", meaning "How can it be that our company is paying you your outrageous fees when you didn't even go to college, for crissakes?!?" I understand. To some executive, who is not totally results oriented, who may be making, say, $100,000 a year, the idea of paying $4,600 a day (the equivalent of $920,000 to $1,650,000 a year, depending on whether you count workdays or calendar days) to somebody who didn't even go to college is troubling. Of course, such executives ought to look around more carefully. They'd see that a whole lot of them, including folks with two and three degrees, are working for a whole lot of us uneducated entrepreneurs!

Nothing Against College.

I have nothing against college, incidentally, as long as the person going understands what it is and what it isn't. For some careers, such as doctors, lawyers, and schoolteachers, it's essential. They have these rules about self-taught brain surgeons. But as I said, for most it is at best preparation only to work for and thus be dependent on someone else. In many respects, it prepares people for an antiquated career model: getting the good job with the good company, climbing that corporate ladder, and staying there for forty years. If you attend a university with very strong, active, loyal alumni, those contacts can be very useful to you in the future, such as in getting a job or getting hired to sell insurance.

To avoid being caught and called a hypocrite, let me tell you that both my stepson and stepdaughter went to college. Marty is an MIT graduate and does things with computers I don't begin to understand. (I use mine as an electric paperweight.) After graduating MIT, he was snapped up by a big company, made very good money working there and at another big company for a few years, but then got the entrepreneurial itch and, with partners, is growing some kind of high-tech company. And having to learn a lot of lessons never mentioned at MIT. Jennifer went to Arizona State, postgrad at Syracuse University, where she attended the prestigious Maxwell School of Public Policy. As I'm writing this, she's working for the National Geographic Society in Washington, D.C., while waiting to leave for a two-year stint in the Peace Corps. To my knowledge, she has no entrepreneurial ambitions. Attending college was probably a very good decision on her part. It was her decision. We neither pushed nor discouraged either of them from doing whatever they wanted to do.

However, let's say that you are reading this book and, like

me, Dave Thomas, or Quentin Tarantino, you never spent time in hallowed, ivy-covered walls. Get over it. That only handicaps you if you want to get hired by a college grad to be a drone in a big company, or if you want to be a brain surgeon, or, otherwise, if you let it be a personal, emotional, self-image-weakening hang-up. When I make a bank deposit, they don't deduct 10 percent because I made all that money without going to college.

Often, when I take calls on radio talk shows, people call in to discuss their ideas for new products and businesses, and bemoan the fact that they do not have a college education, do not have a business background, and therefore do not know (and the implication is: cannot learn) what they need to know to turn their idea into a viable business.

Nuts.

You cannot possibly study the lives of the people I've just described—and the many others just like them—and still cling to "lack of formal education" as a rationale for not accomplishing whatever it is you might want to do.

As far as securing the knowledge you need, I can suggest three courses of action that just about anybody can follow:

One, get to the nearest big city's main public library and befriend the librarians in the business section. I defy you not to find a true wealth of information relevant to any idea, product, service, business, or problem right there at the library—free. There are directories for virtually every purpose. How-to books written by successful leaders of every imaginable field of endeavor. Patent, trademark, and copyright searches can be done there. Manufacturers, importers; suppliers, or manufacturers' representatives, distributors, wholesalers, or other distribution companies can be found there. Statistical data from mailing lists for any conceivable market is readily available. A growing number of libraries are now on-line, on the Internet, too, so you can easily access all kinds of resources they don't have at your particular library.

Two, seek out the fifty smartest, most successful people in your chosen field, wherever they are in the country, and go and buy them breakfast, lunch, or dinner, beg time with them, and pick their brains. (Ten of the fifty will give you some time.) My speaking colleague Jim Rohn calls this "taking a millionaire to lunch." You can also meet these people at trade association meetings and conventions. Have carefully prepared questions based on having thoroughly researched these people. Do as Napoleon Hill did in *Think and Grow Rich:* identify the commonalties, the strategies they *all* use, the characteristics they *all* exhibit.

Three, go to work in the field you wish to exploit, in a company where you can learn a great deal by observation. Consider working free if necessary. (See Chapter 10.) Be a sponge. Soak up everything you can. The individual who pays attention every minute can gain ten years' experience in ten months.

Why Getting Past the Lack-of-Education Bugaboo Is So Important

Here is an actual letter I got:

I'm twenty three years old and frustrated as hell. I hate my job and want to own my own business. Your books really inspired me, but I have one major problem. I'm interested in fitness and nutrition, I study it on my own, and I wish I could create products or a business in this field but I don't have any degrees in it. I am not certified in this area. I'm wondering whether people will take me seriously without a degree in this field.

This young man is imprisoned by an erroneous belief that some authority must somehow "knight" him before he can be taken seriously by the world at large. In the health and fitness field, we have people like Richard Simmons or Jake of "Body by Jake," who have reached millions of people with their encouraging messages and practical methods—but neither of these men have any "official" credentials behind them that I know of. Jean Nidetch, who founded Weight Watchers, now the largest and most respected weight loss assistance organization in America, helping nearly a million people a year, had the following qualifications: She was a fat housewife, a formerly fat bus driver, formerly fat child, who had tried diet after diet after diet—in her own words "made promises in the bathtub and broke them in the kitchen." She had no "credentials" except finally discovering a regimen of eating, thought, and behavior modification that worked. And all of the Weight Watchers group leaders and instructors share only one credential: They've all taken weight off and kept it off following a Weight Watchers regimen.

While the fellow who wrote to me, all tied up by his own lack-of-formal-education inhibitions, is sitting around bemoaning his situation, the next Jean Nidetch or Richard Simmons is emerging, creating a business empire and helping huge numbers of people, also without benefit of official credentials.

From Sleeping in Her Car to Chauffeuring Celebrities

One final story about all this. When I speak at Peter Lowe International's Success Events and share the platform with various celebrities, in every city limos are used to get us speakers from hotel to arena or convention center and back to hotel. In San Jose, I was chauffeured back to my hotel in a classic Rolls-Royce—the kind Gene Barry had on the TV program *Burke's Law*—by an explosively enthusiastic lady named "Flavor" Sabar. She was providing limo service free that day to all the speakers, for an opportunity to meet them and talk with them, maybe picking up a gem or two about how to be more successful in her business. I admired that initiative and was impressed with her dynamic personality, so I asked about her "story." Flavor (real name: Caroline) came from a broken home and poverty in the Detroit inner city. At a young age, she dropped out of school and hitchhiked to California. She worked odd jobs, cleaned houses, and made friends. One helped her get a real estate license. She made friends of rich clients. A couple of them backed her in acquiring the Rolls and a big white Bentley to start her limo service.

"I once lived in an old car. Now here I am driving this beautiful limousine," Flavor says. Her goal is to become a chauffeur to the stars, taking care of an elite clientele of Hollywood celebrities, entertainment industry executives, authors, and speakers. Based on her attitude alone, I would not be at all surprised to catch a glimpse of her letting a famous actress out of her limo at the Oscars some year very soon. And they will not ask her whether or not she has a college degree.

CONTRARIAN SUCCESS STRATEGY:

If you have a good education, by all means make the most of it. But never use lack of formal education as an excuse and never let yourself feel inferior to those with better formal educations. There is abundant proof that you can reach just about any heights in business without college or even a high school education if you will do the things necessary to otherwise obtain the information and master the skills specifically relevant to your objectives.

CHAPTER 4

Modesty and Humility May Be Admirable Qualities in a Monk, but Not in an Entrepreneur

"The meek shall inherit the earth . . . but not in our lifetimes."
—Mike Todd, Hollywood impresario

"Timid salesmen have skinny kids."   Zig Ziglar

Maybe you were raised in a family environment where modesty and humility were taught and valued as virtues. Maybe you were conditioned early on with "speak only when spoken to" . . . "bragging is a sin" . . . "don't blow your own horn" . . . "modesty is a virtue," and so on. I find that this conditioning is inhibiting, even crippling for many people when they enter the competitive, entrepreneurial environment.

When you set out to do something of significance, you will most often meet with massive resistance right from the git-go. Naysayers, doubting Thomases, and critics inside the four walls of your own home, at work, from bankers, vendors, whoever. You will likely be challenged every step of the way. Then, if you get past that, you will find vying for attention in a cluttered marketplace full of jaded, sated consumers tough sledding for the modest and humble. Overcoming all this requires a certain amount of arrogance, believing that you are right even when the world says you are wrong and that you have something important to say even if initially greeted with uninterest.

Arrogance Is an Almost Essential Success Characteristic

Ray DeMarini and Mike Eggiman were profiled in *Success* magazine. They created a new, whizbang kind of bat for softball players. Their first office was a barn with a dirt floor and no heat—although, DeMarini mentioned, "Every once in a while we'd feel the hot breath of a cow standing behind us." They had no money to buy manufacturing equipment, so they had to make their own. After first year's sales of $65,000, they applied for a $109,000 SBA loan. "The SBA guys asked me why I thought I could compete against $100 million companies," recalled DeMarini. "I looked at them real serious and said, 'What makes you think they can compete against me?' " They got the loan. And that's exactly the kind of arrogance I'm talking about. .

By the way, their company's 1995 sales hit $2.5 million, and they recently obtained a million dollars of additional financing to create a full-scale manufacturing facility.

I had an almost identical experience a number of years ago, when I was negotiating the takeover of a very troubled company, sitting in the office of the president of the bank, discussing assuming liability for the company's near half million dollars of debt. He looked at me and said: "I don't see anything in your résumé that qualifies you to run this company. What makes you think you are smart enough to turn it around?" I answered: "I would have been smart enough not to let them get into me for a half million dollars in the first place." I didn't make a friend, but I closed the deal. That's the kind of arrogance I'm talking about.

If you are not prepared to look anybody and everybody in the eye without blinking and tell them that you are the best at what you do and that you know your stuff, somebody's going to kick your butt and send you home early. And if you are not going to knock down doors, holler at the top of your lungs, make a miserable pest out of yourself, and do whatever else is necessary to attract attention and get your message across, the marketplace will simply pass you by.

I have reluctantly learned the importance and value of self-promotion. It doesn't much matter whether you are a speaker and consultant like me, a chiropractor, a hair stylist, or the CEO of a huge corporation, it turns out that people prefer to do business with VERY confident individuals unabashed about proclaiming, as Muhammad Ali did, "I am the greatest." Way back in 1964, Ali, then Cassius Clay, said, "Ain't never been another fighter like me. Ain't never been no *nothing* like me." What do you say about yourself, to yourself, when you look in the mirror? And what do you say about yourself—with conviction—to the world?

This is pretty obvious, I suppose. But it also links to another, very big problem for a lot of business owners, entrepreneurs, salespeople, consultants, doctors, other professionals, and service providers: reluctance to charge what their time and expertise is worth, guilt and insecurity about their fees or prices, and anxiety about asking to be paid.

The Number One Hang-up

Over the years, I have watched countless different kinds of businesspeople underprice their products and services or procrastinate endlessly over making obviously, painfully necessary price increases. I have seen artists, writers, craftspeople, consultants, doctors, every imaginable expert 100 percent confident of his expertise but 100 percent chicken when it comes to setting prices and asking customers, clients, or patients to pay those prices. I think more people have more hang-ups about asking for money than about any other subject.

Some years ago, I advised a client providing a particular specialized service to raise his fee from the $500 a day he was getting to $2,500 a day in one leap. Against the will of every fiber in his being, and in dry-mouth fear, he did just that, and announced his new fee to his clients and his marketplace. He lost only a few clients but gained better replacements, and heard grumbling from only a few more; most continued to hire him without complaint; a few asked why he had waited so long to start charging what his service was obviously worth!

He was not and is not alone. His fear of asking for what he perceived as a very large amount of money is all too common.

There is also a lot of yakking about "giving." Many people like to talk about the idea of "giving" of expertise, time, and service and then believing that will somehow come back to you. I happen to believe in "giving" of yourself as well as your money to worthwhile individuals and organizations in your community; that's charity. And it is spiritually restorative. It is even profitable. Charitable giving with no intent of personal gain is proven to return dividends to the givers. However, the same "giving attitude" in the business world will, more often than not, wind up with extending a hand and pulling back a bloody stump.

In business, you must do everything you can to protect your ideas, information, and interests and to obtain full, maximum compensation for your knowledge and expertise. The respect granted you is the respect you command and demand.

Of course, you want to go the extra mile in delivering greater service than your customers could possibly have expected. Of course, you want to provide your employees with every possible opportunity to excel, advance, and feel rewarded. But that is simply prudent investment. It's not giving. Do not confuse the two.

You NEVER want to give away knowledge, expertise, or your time.

Don't Undervalue What Is "Common Knowledge" to You but Very Uncommon Knowledge to the Other Guy

Mark McCormack created the International Management Group with $1,000 and a handshake, then guided it to its current status: a multimillion-dollar, global corporation leading in the professional representation and management of athletes and entertainers as well as commercially sponsored, made-for-TV sports events. *Sports Illustrated* magazine called Mark "the most powerful man in sports." I've appeared as a speaker on several programs with Mark McCormack, and I'm always impressed with the down-to-earth practicality of his advice.

In his book *What They Don't Teach You at Harvard Business School*, Mark wrote about his own learning curve on this issue: "Many companies fail to place a premium on the real dollar worth of their expertise, or what it would cost an outsider to learn what they already know. So did we for about ten years. During that time we had been involved with more than a thousand companies in one sports promotion or another. We had amassed an enormous body of knowledge as to how companies should go about realizing their marketing goals through sports. And we often gave away this knowledge. If a company signed on John Newcombe, for example, and then didn't know how to use him, for everyone's sake we had to step in and show them.

"By the early 1970s we recognized that more and more companies wanted to get into sports but had no idea how to do it . . . We finally began charging for our expertise. Today, our consulting division is our fastest growing company. . . . If companies took the time to realize the true worth of their expertise, they could use it for growth opportunities which might otherwise be overlooked: as a separate profit center, such as we made of our consulting division; as an add-on to goods or services; as a sales incentive."

But you cannot use it for any of those things if you give it away.

One of my favorite metaphysical authors, Stuart Wilde, says, "If they show up, bill 'em." It is my experience that people do not—and maybe they cannot—place value on or extract value from advice, ideas, information, or services given to them free of charge. So the less of that you do, the better for everybody. As of this writing, I charge $4,700 a day or $700 an hour for my consulting. I will engage in a brief telephone conversation preparatory to consulting with someone who has qualified as a potential client, but that's it. I will no longer even go to lunch with somebody seeking information from me for free. If they show up, I charge 'em. And the tougher I have gotten about all this, the more I have prospered.

How Much Are You Worth?

We are conditioned to think in terms of X dollars per hour.

This is undoubtedly how you were paid in your first job or first few jobs. It may still be the way you are paid now. Or, even if you are a salaried employee, I'll bet that occasionally you mentally convert your paycheck into dollars per hour as sort of a checkup on how well you are doing. Even distributorships, business opportunities, and franchises are often sold by talking about income in terms of dollars per hour. And this is deeply ingrained in many people. It is also very limiting.

Every once in a while it still occurs to me that my $700 an hour base fee is a helluva lot of money. But then I force that out of my mind. To some clients, I'm worth $700 a minute. In every instance, I'm worth more than I charge. A true bargain. Because the value of expertise must be measured by its impact, not by the time required to dispense it.

You cannot measure Emmitt Smith's or Michael Jordan's salaries in terms of yards run or baskets made. Their impact on their teams is much greater than that. They impact ticket sales revenue, television revenue, merchandise sales, championships won that increase team value, and many other things. And they are paid based on all of that impact. In fact, when a check is written out to a Michael Jordan for $10 million it really is for zero. It costs more to pay the $500,000-a-year journeyman player than to pay a Jordan his due.

Mark McCormack tells the story of Picasso, asked in a restaurant to scribble something on a napkin; the woman offered to pay whatever it was worth. He scribbled and asked "$10,000."

"But it only took thirty seconds," she protested.

"No," Picasso replied. "*Forty years* and thirty seconds."

Same here. Sometimes it takes me days of hard work to write a sales letter for a client. But often it does not. Often I can assemble a sales letter in a few hours, yet my fee will be $8,400 or more. But if it took three hours, it really took twenty years and three hours. And even that is less relevant than the fact that it would have taken the client three months to get a comparable result done internally. And even that is less relevant than the fact that he will mail millions of the letter and make hundreds of thousands of dollars by doing so.

You may be like many people—you may feel you do not have any expertise that is worth any serious money. Odds are, you're wrong. When I teach people how to become consultants, I point out that there are over two thousand different consulting specialties and that just about everybody has some kind of education, experience, or expertise that can provide the basis for a consulting practice. Just for example, I know a woman who stayed at home and raised four kids, including a pair of twins, then wanted to go back out into the workplace. She was such an efficient, highly organized person—out of necessity, obviously—she began consulting, going into homes and sometimes offices and helping people get organized, at $150 an hour. With no résumé and a high school education, in the regular job market she'd have been lucky to get an entry-level job with about $150 a week in take-home pay. But by recognizing the real value of her expertise, she's been able to earn that much per hour.

But what if you are not a consultant like me—or her—and don't want to be? What if you are a clothing salesman in a menswear store? If you are smart, you will maximize your value by becoming truly, genuinely expert in assisting men at looking their very best, by choosing the right colors, patterns, and fabrics for the right person, by being able to perfectly coordinate suits, shirts, ties, and shoes, and by being the most knowledgeable individual around on fashion trends. All of that is certainly worth a hundred or two hundred dollars an hour. No, you may not be able to directly charge for it. But, as Mark McCormack points out, you can use it as added value, as an incentive for clients to do business with you and return to you every single time they are ready to purchase clothing. You can write a book, *10 Great Tips to Look Your Best*, you can put out a monthly newsletter for your customers and local media, you can position yourself as a "Professional Image Consultant," you can lecture to local groups, get on talk shows; and you WILL be perceived differently by your customers. You can begin training your customers to call you for an appointment rather than just dropping in. You can gain such control over your loyal clientele that you become a "franchise player" to your employer, so you can work four day weeks instead of five and make just as much money. You can sell or value-add a complete wardrobe analysis and consultation, via home visits. And you will change your life.

If you are going to achieve exceptional success, especially exceptional financial success, you have to break completely free of wage-earner thinking and comparison about what you charge and what you make.

CONTRARIAN SUCCESS STRATEGY:

Give to charity but never give in business. Place the highest possible value on your expertise and confidently present that value to the world. When they show up, charge 'em. The meek and the humble may be very talented and capable but will all too often be overlooked or undervalued. Arrogance and self-promotion are necessary to advance in just about any business environment.

CHAPTER 5

"Mind Your Manners"—or Is Being Rude, Aggressive, Rough-Around-the-Edges One of the Great Unsung Secrets of Success?

"Leona Helmsley is a truly evil human being."
　　　　　　　—Donald Trump, in a *Playboy* magazine
　　　　　　　interview, March 1990

"Donald Trump is a snake."
　　　　　　　—Leona Helmsley, in a *Playboy* magazine
　　　　　　　interview, November 1990.

Because I routinely recommend it as "must reading," a lot of people have told me over the years that they have never read Robert Ringer's book *Winning Through Intimidation* because they are offended or turned off by the title, by the very idea of intimidation.

I suppose we have all been raised with the "politeness ethic." I know that I was. And I have often been chided and cautioned about being too aggressive, abrasive, arrogant. Warned about losing my temper. Urged to avoid offending others at any cost. It turns out this may be some really terrible advice.

Is He an Egotistical Blowhard in Buckskin or America's Greatest Contemporary Trial Lawyer with Rare Insights into the Human Condition?

I have met and had opportunities to chat privately with Gerry Spence, as we have appeared as speakers at a number of events. Spence is the buckskin-jacketed defense lawyer with the "aw, shucks" country boy persona whose fame multiplied during the O. J. trial, as Spence appeared regularly on Larry King's show as chief pundit, then got his own CNBC cable talk show.

Randy Weaver. Ruby Ridge. Cause célèbre for the militia movements. On April 13, 1994, Randy Weaver walked into a Boise, Idaho, courtroom facing charges of murdering a U.S. marshal during the siege, owning and selling illegal weapons, conspiracy, and a few other crimes, and he was already convicted in the media and in the public eye, with his actual courtroom conviction viewed as little more than a tiresome little formality to be taken care of. But for forty-two days, Gerry Spence defended Randy Weaver. Prosecuted the FBI and the federal government. Mesmerized the jury with the kind of courtroom tactics and dramatics more typical of old Perry Mason black-and-white TV show reruns than real life. The jury acquitted Weaver of all charges. Gerry Spence also won a $3.1 million damage award for Weaver from the federal government. It was a typical Spence case: the misunderstood, oppressed, victimized "little guy" against big government run amok or a big, callous corporation. It's a role he is familiar with, comfortable with, and passionate about. And he has yet to lose any such high-profile case.

My own experiences with Gerry Spence, limited though they may be, have been fascinating to me. When he comes into "the green room," the speakers' waiting room backstage at a seminar, his presence takes over the room. He is larger than life. In keeping with every criticism I've ever read of him, his ego seems larger than life too. Backstage he is attention commanding and attention greedy. Onstage, while holding an audience of fifteen thousand in his hand, and coming across as most humble, there is still also arrogance—the first time we were on a program together, he deliberately ignored the meeting planner's instructions and the huge, blinking digital timer and went a whopping twenty minutes over his allotted time. The second time, given stern instructions, the flashing timer, and a staff person pacing in front of the stage at his cutoff time, he did wind up, but he let the audience know he was being "forced" to cut his remarks short and that he wasn't pleased about it. Yet, he has personally been very courteous and gracious to me. And I must tell you: He delivers the goods. His speech is excellent and meaningful. His book *How to Argue and Win Every Time* is so good I bought copies for my Gold Inner Circle Members (VIP newsletter subscribers). If I was in big legal trouble, I'd want Gerry Spence, insufferable ego be damned.

Things like this cause many to view him as arrogant: showing off his huge, *Architectural Digest*–featured home, he told a *Playboy* interviewer, "You see this house and whatever else I have. It all comes from insurance companies. That's like an Indian hangin' out his scalps. These are my f—ing scalps."

Spence is gentle when playing to an audience, in person, to twelve or twelve thousand, or on TV. But in individual relationships, in conducting business behind the scenes, he is anything but gentle. I cannot imagine anybody intimidating Gerry Spence. I can imagine Spence intimidating a lot of people.

They Set Fire to Dale Carnegie's How to Win Friends and Influence People and Still Succeeded

In 1996, Dennis Rodman was a champion without a team. Only Zen-coach Phil Jackson at the Chicago Bulls decided to gamble on Rodman, and he admits to misgivings. It's no wonder. That much-tattooed, weird-colored-hair Rodman either frightens or irritates virtually everybody he deals with. He describes himself as cynical, self-centered, and authority hating. He'd flunk the Dale Carnegie course big-time. If Will

Rogers were alive, he could say, "I never met a man I didn't like, until I met Dennis Rodman." Yet here he is, at the top of his game, on the best team in the NBA, making megamoney, and if he is careful at all with some of his money, set for life. And, to the amazement of many, the public likes Rodman's bad-boy brashness. Proof? After his Pizza Hut spot in March 1995, sales of the stuffed crust pizza leaped up by 15 percent.

Many people find Deion Sanders's arrogance and self-aggrandizement very pushy self-promotion. He is a man of many faces: The brash, flamboyant self-aggrandizer festooned in gold rope necklaces and dazzling shades hides a non-smoking, nondrinking homebody who prefers a quiet evening with his wife and kids than a showy night on the town club hopping. And behind all the dazzle and hype is the most versatile, exciting, and one of the highest paid, richest professional athletes in pro sports, for good reason. In 1995, Deion was named the NFL's Defensive Player of the Year by the Associated Press. He is the first athlete to participate in both baseball's World Series and the NFL's play-off games. It was Sanders who once left a Falcons football game at Miami, jumped into a limo, hopped on a jet, and arrived in Pittsburgh in time to play in a Braves baseball play-off game—lowered from the sky by helicopter, Deion, the hero, the superstar. About all the self-promotion, Deion says, "I saw that quarterbacks make a lot of money, running backs make a lot of money, cornerbacks don't make a lot of money. I'm a cornerback, so I figure I've gotta do more than the usual to get my mother her dream home. Bing! 'Prime Time.'" (His mother worked as a cleaning woman, his father a mostly unemployed drug addict. Most of his childhood friends joined gangs or sold drugs and are now dead or in prison.)

Even those who hate Deion's hype love to watch Deion perform. And there is not a peer who won't give him grudging respect. Ram receiver Isaac Bruce is one of many who has actually been coached on the field by Sanders. Lined up opposite Bruce, Deion gave him advice on how to run his routes better and make it more difficult to defend him, but he also held him to zero receptions for the whole game. "Instead of giving me a hard time, he's kind of coaching me. He's saying, 'Look, you need to stay low when coming out of your cuts, so I won't be able to tell where you're going.' " Writing in *Sports Illustrated* about this, John Ed Bradley noted, "To offer advice to your own teammates is one thing; to give it to the player you are trying to stop reveals a self-confidence that is downright spooky."

Deion Sanders is many things, including being the brashest, most confident, flashiest, most promotional, hype-iest, pushiest player in the NFL.

Pushy people getting ahead is certainly not isolated to the world of sports. The number of businesspeople who defy the "smile, listen, be nice, be pleasant, go along to get along" idea is legion.

Donald Trump, just as an example. From a little scene at his incredibly expensive Mar-a-Lago private club and resort home in Florida, where The Donald is simultaneously giving two interviews, one to a reporter from *Paris Match* magazine doing a profile titled "The Comeback of the Decade," the other to a writer preparing the pages on Trump to be included in the glitzy, hardbound *Gold Coast Guest Informant* book stuck inside all the upscale hotel rooms in south Florida, here are a few Trumpisms:

In response to one of the interviewer's questions, Trump calls out to Marla, "Honey, what don't I like about myself?" Then there is a pointed silence from both of them as they try to think of something.

Describing his attack on New York City real estate, Trump says, "I wasn't satisfied to make a good living. I was looking to make a statement."

About Trump Tower: "It is THE most successful apartment building in the United States."

Donald Trump has a reputation among ex-employees as an unbending, outrageously demanding man who flaunts his wealth and power. Among those he has done deals with, Trump is known as having a steel-tough preference for "I win, you lose" rather than "win-win" beneath his gracious public persona. He has had plenty of controversy during his flamboyant career. The media scorched him over the Merv Griffin deal and scorched him worse during his ugly divorce from

Ivana. He flirted with bankruptcy when the real estate market went south at the beginning of the nineties. As recently as 1995, he was still lugging around over $100 million of personally guaranteed debt, but in April 1996, New Jersey state regulators approved a $1.4 billion merger of Trump's two biggest casino properties, instantly reducing Trump's debt load by $65 million. Some say: Trump dodged another bullet. His continuing 1980s-style conspicuous consumption offends many. His arrogance seems to offend just about everybody.

A much repeated joke originated by a Trump "insider" reveals how some close to him feel about his ego. Trump is in an elevator. Just as the doors are about to close, a young, gorgeous, curvaceous woman slips in. She says, "I know you. You're Donald Trump, one of the richest men in the world. We're alone in this elevator. Right here, right now, I could strip naked and we could have wild, spontaneous, passionate, animal sex." Trump thinks about this and then asks, "But what's in it for me?" A Trump associate told me the unsanitized version of that joke with great glee.

He is certainly no poster boy for "how to win friends and influence people." Still, one cannot argue with Trump's abilities to bounce back from adversity, pull off astounding deals, and keep succeeding over and over again. Like that bunny in the battery commercials, Trump keeps going. And going. And going.

One of the things I find most intriguing about Trump is how consistent he is. When things are going well or when things are going badly, Trump seems never embarrassed or cowed, always supremely confident, and always promotional. In his second book, *Trump: Surviving at the Top*, he wrote: "I have a reputation for being tough, and I'd like to think it's justified. You must be tough when a lot of influential people are saying that your day has come and gone, when your marriage is breaking up, and when business pressures are increasing. . . . Toughness, as I see it, is a quality made up of equal parts of strength, intelligence and self-respect. . . . Occasionally, toughness does involve some old-fashioned ass kicking. There are times, for example, when on the spur of the moment I'll dial the number of one of my hotels just to see how long it takes for my people to answer the phone. If I have to wait for more than five or six rings, I'll tell the employee who finally does answer who I am. Then I'll ask, without hiding my annoyance, what the problem is. . . . I admire toughness in people such as Rupert Murdoch, Steve Ross, Ron Perelman, Marty Davis of Paramount and others. Those are men who expect to succeed and who understand the ins and outs of maintaining success, but they don't feel out of their element when things aren't going well; they are capable of taking a losing proposition and turning it around. . . . The opposite of toughness—weakness—makes me mad and sometimes turns my stomach." Just reading these lines, you get a feel for a Donald Trump you'd rather be on the right side than the wrong side of.

Still, Donald Trump looks mild compared to Jerry Jones.

Jerry Jones came from Texas's rival state, Oklahoma, bought the Dallas Cowboys, and promptly, clumsily, gracelessly fired the legendary Tom Landry, immediately raising the ire of season ticket holders, fans, players, the media, and a few million other Texans. He hired an untested college coach with an ego nearly as big as his own—changing the explanation about the hole in the roof of Texas Stadium from the familiar "so God can look down and watch his favorite team play" to "so the sides can stretch and expand to accommodate Jones's and Johnson's egos." This further angered Texas.

Jones said, "This isn't a law firm or a medical practice. It's a football team. And in order to take it out of its nosedive and bring it back up again, I had to find the best qualified management available. And that was me."

After the Jones-Johnson leadership took the Cowboys to winning two Super Bowls and returned the Cowboys to glory, and won forgiveness for Jones, he, in a fit of ego, canned Johnson and replaced him with another college coach, this one also egotistical and bombastic, but also highly controversial, and also from Oklahoma—again enraging the fans and stunning the media.

Jerry Jones has also managed to piss off most of the other NFL owners he shares the cash cow we call "pro football" with, challenging one of the key, cornerstone tenets of the league, revenue sharing, and going outside the league to cut incredibly lucrative sponsorship deals with major corporations. Jones suggests that other owners are lazy and incompetent when it comes to marketing their teams. In just a few short years, Jones has managed to dislodge and replace Al Davis as THE black sheep of the NFL, and that is no small accomplishment.

And Jones could apparently care less.

Jones, incidentally, seems to like other brash self-promoters. He ponied up a whopping $35 million to take Deion Sanders away from the 49ers.

There have been even less pleasant yet successful CEOs. When W. Michael Blumenthal was CEO of the Bendix Corporation—in the early 1970s, a $2 billion-a-year operation—he acquired a reputation as an arrogant, aggressive, tough guy, all too often so hurried as to be blatantly rude. A *Fortune* magazine profile began: "Visitors to the Bendix Corporation headquarters should be advised not to stand near any closed doors. There is too much danger that they will be knocked flat by W. Michael Blumenthal. . . . Blumenthal doesn't just enter a room—he explodes into it, and a bruising bump awaits anyone who happens to be in his way." When you study interviews that were done with Blumenthal and articles written about him, you get a clear picture of a man viewed as rude and abrasive by others, but viewed by himself as a man holding a temper in check, committed to results, under constant pressure, and unable to take time for patience with incompetence or social niceties. Blumenthal even questioned himself—often—for being too "soft."

Blumenthal later salvaged the near-dead Sperry Corporation and created Unisys.

A favorite Blumenthalism: "It takes intelligence and ingenuity and years of application to ruin a large corporation."

Henry Ford II was described by *Fortune* magazine as inspiring "respect, awe and sometimes downright fear." In 1995, when I met with Lee Iacocca (for my client, the Guthy-Renker Corporation), I found him to be a very pleasant, gracious, thoughtful man, yet I also had a sense of great impatience being held tightly in check, and I had the thought:

This is not a guy you would want to get on the wrong side of. Other people at this same meeting were, quite frankly, clearly intimidated by Iacocca, even though he made no overt effort to intimidate.

Many successful people DO overtly intimidate.

When I was in the advertising agency business, I dealt with the owner of one of the most successful auto dealerships in northeastern Ohio. He had a reputation for "taking no crap" and for throwing his weight around. It was earned. When you went to his office, you got a first-class lesson in blatant intimidation. You took a private elevator up to a second floor built on top of the showroom. When you stepped out of the elevator, this guy was barely visible at his desk, on a raised platform, about a mile away from where you were—or so it seemed. He happened to be a world traveler and "great white hunter," so your walk toward his desk took you past a variety of unusual, impressive artifacts and life-size taxidermied exotic, fierce animals. A fountain and fully stocked pond. Finally, you stepped up onto the platform and took a seat in one of the two chairs facing his desk. Both were too small, with too-short legs, and the front legs slightly shorter than the back. No side table, causing many salespeople to try and operate with their attaché cases open and precariously balanced on their laps. The guy's desk was huge, carved out of a giant tree trunk. His chair was on a hidden platform, about a step higher than everything else. He made you battle for his attention, taking phone calls, signing documents, barking instructions out on his intercom while you tried to deal with him. He reduced many people to blubber.

I got to know him reasonably well and came to understand the thinking behind his behavior. First off, he had built his entire business with woefully little capital, as the youngest auto dealership owner in that company, in all of North America, with no industry experience. He figured that everybody would view him as weak, vulnerable, and easy to "snow" unless he struck fear into their hearts from minute one. Second, he got where he got by being very, very tough and wanted to do business only with people just as tough as he was. He respected and quickly trusted the few people who were unimpressed with his "show" and who stood up to him. But those he drove off, he wrote off.

Nice Girls Finish Last

In *Sports Illustrated*, Shelley Smith wrote, "She's big. She's bad. She's obnoxious and caustic." Ms. Smith was describing Nanci Donnellan, better known as The Sports Babe, the first woman to host a nationally syndicated daily sports radio talk show. For four hours a day, five days a week, sports fans dial up 1-800-SAY-BABE and, more often than not, are treated to courtesy comparable to that of a bona fide New York deli; something along the lines of "Yeah, whaddya want?"

The Babe has IDd the city of Portland, Oregon, as "the plumber's butt of America," she cuts callers off for any reason or no reason, and may very well be the most annoying, argued with, and argued about sports commentator since Howard Cosell. She has also fought with bosses and radio station owners on her way up.

She is just one of many very successful women described by others as tough, obnoxious, difficult, having chips on their shoulders, being ball-busters, and so on. Barbra Streisand comes instantly to mind. Comedian and sitcom star Brett Butler survived a physically abusive marriage, the grind of doing stand-up comedy in joints from one end of the country to another, and the challenge of delivering material that turned off as many people as it turned on. She was turned down for a comedy special by HBO because they viewed her as "too dark, political and mean."

Her ABC sitcom *Grace Under Fire* was an instant hit, but Brett fought with the writers and producers and has developed a reputation in the industry as "a difficult woman." Her show's creator and first producer, Chuck Lorre, quit after just one season, blaming Brett for making "what should have been a joy, a living hell." Other frequently turned-over writers and staffers complain about her mood swings and hysterical outbursts. An agent who represents people who have worked on the show told *Playboy* magazine, "Brett makes Roseanne seem like Snow White."

She told *TV Guide*, "I don't care how difficult they said I was this year. You're damned if you fight for quality or you're run out of the business if you don't." Nobody's going to run her out of the business.

Say What You Will— She Runs a Helluva Hotel

Leona Helmsley is one of the most demonized entrepreneurs of our time. Ex-employees surfaced with all sorts of wicked witch stories. Letterman made jokes. Well, as her ads say, say what you will, she runs a helluva hotel. Let me tell you my favorite, personal Leona Helmsley story. I have never met her. But I have spoken with her on the phone.

I had arrived at one of her hotels late in the afternoon to set up for a seminar that evening. With displays to set up, the need to shower and dress, I didn't have a minute to spare. But disaster had struck. The hotel had moved us from the preassigned meeting room to a basement hellhole. Nothing was set up as it was supposed to be. And the banquet manager was 110 percent uncooperative. Resistant. In short order, she and I were mortal enemies. My blood pressure was through the roof. I had ripped a phone from the meeting room wall and thrown a chair. The banquet manager had retreated to her office only after ensuring that no one on the entire hotel staff would lift a finger at my request. From the front desk's courtesy phone, I called New York and got put through to Leona Helmsley. I told her my story. She said, "It will be taken care of. Put the front desk manager on the phone with me."

I stood there and watched the blood drain out of his face.

Ten minutes later, an army had materialized to attend to my needs. A meeting room was transformed at lightning speed.

The next morning, the new front desk manager asked me what had gone on there. I asked him what he knew. "Not much," he said, "except that everybody on this staff was fired. Our whole crew here today was flown in from New York last night to take their place." Wow.

And for the most part, the Helmsley hotels are the most consistently outstanding properties I know of, with the Four Seasons hotels in neck-and-neck competition.

Say what you will, she RUNS a helluva hotel.

"Why Good Girls Don't Get Ahead but Gutsy Girls Do"

That's the title of a book by Kate White, who has been editor-in-chief of *Working Woman* magazine, *McCall's*, and now *Redbook*. In her book, she tells of qualifying as one of ten college students to compete for a *Glamour* magazine cover. All ten were taken to racks of clothes and invited to pick out clothes to wear for their photo shoot. Even though warm "earth tones" were in that year and the others chose those clothes, Kate recalls making a beeline for a bright yellow turtleneck sweater. "I wondered guiltily if I should warn the others that magazine covers are usually bold and colorful," Kate says, "but I kept my lips zipped." She got the cover, the cover got her noticed, and that got her a job at *Glamour* after graduation.

"To a good girl," she notes, "*that* kind of success is the antithesis of the work ethic and all the other principles she lives by. A good girl believes that success *should* be based on the quality of her work, *not* on how she looks or sounds, so when rewards are handed to someone who simply talks a good game—or worse, simply looks the part—she's appalled. . . . But the truth is, paying your dues by accomplishing certain goals *doesn't* necessarily get you into the club you want to join. You have to look and sound like you deserve to be a member."

Is this an advocacy for no-talent, no-work self-promotion based on image alone? Not at all. But Kate White IS giving sage if often unwelcome advice: that you cannot get ahead based on how things *should* work; you have to get ahead based on how things *actually* work.

In her book, Kate goes on to give career women plenty of solid, practical advice, much of it contrary to what their mothers, friends, and peers would give.

She's Pushy, but . . .

I happen to have a client, a woman, who is a vice-president in a company that is very much an "old boys' club" in an industry that is very much an "old boys' club." I'm not going to identify her or her industry here. But suffice it to say, top-level women executives are as rare there as hen's teeth. On several visits to the company's home office and at several conferences, I've had conversations with her peers, other executives at the company, her subordinates, the sales professionals she supervises—ALL men. In almost every case, their comments begin like this: "She's a pushy broad, but . . ."—and the rest is grudgingly complimentary.

She's a pushy broad, but she gets the job done. She's a pushy broad, but she knows her stuff. She's a pushy broad, but—and so on.

It's very clear to me that if she wasn't a "pushy broad," she'd have never made it to veep in this company.

Kate White advises, for example, to dress as if you were in the job you aspire to. "Sure, a few co-workers will give you a Who-Does-She-Think-She-Is? look when you walk in wearing an expensive suit that you spent your last dime on. But the people making the decisions will be impressed." Also: Master and use confident body language. Also: When you talk, cut to the chase. Also: Clearly ask for what you want. Don't be bashful or subtle. Also: Be your own PR agent. "Never say 'I was lucky.' Make yourself a legend in your own time. In this case, becoming a legend means creating a wonderful mystique about your personality and career. Successful legends do this by perpetuating certain 'truths' about themselves until an oral history comes into existence and is brought up whenever their names are mentioned."

I know this to be VERY good counsel, because every highly successful woman I know has lived it on the way up.

In Sports, Tough Guys Win

Cincinnati University basketball coach Bob Huggins has received as many as twenty technical fouls in a single season. His sideline behavior is dubbed by many as outrageous and obnoxious, rivaling Indiana's Bobby Knight. But that pales in comparison to what he is like at practice. He routinely throws players out of practice for not working hard enough. He drives his players relentlessly. He has fought with just about everybody: officials, college administrators, his players, and the media. He is also famous for taking chances with high-risk kids. One of his stars was once charged with assault for punching a police officer's horse in the nose.

In 1996, he again took Cincinnati to the Final Four— restoring supercharged excitement to a basketball program that had virtually disappeared into oblivion under its former coach. During the summer of 1995, he was rumored in the running for every high-profile opening, including head coach of the NBA's Miami Heat—a job ultimately taken by Pat Riley— until Huggins signed a ten-year contract extension at Cincinnati. He is arguably one of the least liked, most respected, most controversial, and most successful coaches in basketball.

The coaching ranks always include some of these supertough guys. Woody Hayes, Ohio State. Frank Kush, Arizona State University. Both fired after incidents involving physically hitting players. But both were leaders of winning programs and both revered by most of their players. In the NFL, Vince Lombardi, Paul Brown, and Mike Ditka were well known as tough, violent tempered, confrontive coaches hated by some players but loved by others and respected by most. Intimidation. Arrogance. Self-aggrandizement. Rarely presented as virtues. Yet quite possibly essential and inarguably helpful in achieving exceptional levels of success.

So What About Me?

When I started in speaking, I was told by many never to tell a joke that might offend anybody and never to talk about politics, religion, or sex. After a very short time, it dawned on me there wasn't anything of importance left to talk about and, if you never risked telling a joke that might offend somebody, you can't tell a joke, period. If I stuck with that advice, I'd be so bland I'd be invisible. As I've matured as a speaker, I've gotten more and more bombastic, pushy, and risk-taking. Sprinkled throughout my presentations are one-liners and quick shots at liberals, insurance agents, Avon ladies, Jehovah's Witnesses, academics, plumbers, and an assortment of other constituencies often found in my audiences. Every once in a while, somebody complains about being personally offended or about finding me, in general, obnoxious. That's when I know I got it right.

In business, I've had to fight for what I wanted and for what I know to be right just about every step of the way.

Maybe you've noticed: Controversy seems to follow "stars" or standouts in every field. It certainly has followed me. In one association I belong to, I have clients who swear by me, critics who swear at me, I've had allegations made against me to its ethics committee, been expelled, sued the association, been reinstated, and, today, ten years or so after those incidents, the mention of my name still tends to get only the strongest of reactions, pro or con. In the "success" field, as a speaker and an author, titles of my presentations and books—notably *The No B.S., No Holds Barred, Take No Prisoners, Kick Butt and Make Tons of Money Business Success Book*—have sparked controversy. Some have taken the "No B.S." out of context and, with zero sense of humor, used it to accuse me of being unchristian, offensive to Christians, profane. (Not my intent.) Others have focused on the "tons of money" and been offended by that. And THIS book is certain to offend many of my speaking colleagues, those who make their living by unthinkingly, robotically parroting the same old success dogma.

To Be a Chameleon or Not to Be a Chameleon

In recent years, there has been a rash of books, seminars, training programs for salespeople, and the like teaching techniques akin to chameleonism. These suggest altering your entire personality to "match" or "mirror" the person or people you are dealing with at the moment. A little bit of this is useful. There is logic to modifying your selling or communicating "style" to be most acceptable to the other person. But you can certainly carry it too far. Politicians do this to the nth degree, which largely accounts for how little respect anybody has for any of them. If you say "Will the real Bill Clinton stand up?", there's nobody who can. You may win some temporary victories with this approach, but after changing your colors so many times, will you have any true colors left? The contrarian approach: presenting a consistent personality, being yourself, saying what you mean, meaning what you say, and having everybody know it is more likely to lead to lasting, satisfying success.

In fact, there is abundant proof that a maverick, unconventional, even odd style can lead to success.

One of the great speakers, Bill Gove, tells this story from his days in sales at 3M. Bill says that shortly after he got started, his boss called him in and said, "I want you to go down to New Orleans and see our man in the field there, Harry. You've never met anybody like him. He's about sixty pounds overweight, his clothes look like a bulletin board for whatever he ate at lunch, he garbles his words, and he writes up his orders on the back of a napkin."

Bill asked, "So what do you want me to do? Buy him a copy of *Dress for Success*? Fire him?"

Bill's boss said, "Find out what this guy is eating and make sure he gets all he wants. And get some for yourself. Harry's our number one producer."

These days there's a whole lot less tolerance for the Harrys in most big sales organizations. That's understandable, although in some ways a shame. But if you are an entrepreneur, you can be as tolerant of the maverick in you as you wish.

I violate all sorts of business rules. Just for example, I am deliberately difficult for prospective clients to get to. It's even somewhat difficult for my customers to do business with my company: We only answer the phones "live" during specific hours on Tuesday and Thursday; we're on voice mail the rest of the time. Most businesspeople litter the landscape with their business cards. Not me. I annoy a few people after every speaking engagement because I do not carry or use business cards. People come to me after a speech and ask for a card. I tell them I don't use them. If they press—"Why not?"—I explain: "If, after hearing my best hour, you are not interested enough in what I've said to go to the back of the hall and buy my package of books and cassettes, which have my address, phone number, and fax number in them, why on earth would I want you to have my number and clutter up my office with calls or faxes?" Obnoxious. Maybe. But it works for me. And since I'm in charge, I can be as tolerant of such behavior as I choose.

Just the other day, after a speech, one young man muttered as he walked away from me, "You're very rude. I can't imagine how you can be as successful as you are." But that IS a secret of success: Only to the degree that you are willing to risk offending, and actually offend people, can you then have impact on them. I do say things on the platform that offend some people. I do say things person-to-person that some find offensive. But, on the other hand, those are the very same things that have truly profound impact on certain people.

How Much More Offensive Can You Be?

The two biggest figures in broadcasting, as I write this book, are Howard Stern and Rush Limbaugh. I certainly do not need to tell you that Howard Stern offends somebody with almost every word uttered.

Rush Limbaugh was fired in 1984 from a Kansas City radio station for delivering overly controversial, conservative commentaries. He got hired by a Sacramento station to replace Morton Downey Jr., and was told by management, "We're not afraid of controversy here. But we will not back you up if you say things you don't believe. If you can convince us why you believe something, no matter how outrageous it seems, we'll back you up all day long. But we will not have controversy just for the sake of it." Rush says that policy stayed with him and forged his career from that point forward. By his own estimate, Rush mightily offends 40 percent to 50 percent of the people with his current topical, conservative daily broadcasts. And you rarely find anybody who is lukewarm. People either hate or love Limbaugh. Offending those he offends and winning over those who agree with him has made him a multimillion-dollar media personality with the power to make his own books instant best-sellers, to literally "make" little-known products into marketplace giants—like Snapple beverages, Uggs slippers, and some say to have made the Newt Gingrich–Republican takeover of the House in 1995 possible.

Limbaugh exemplifies one of my pet marketing theories: that your ability to create fierce loyalty and enthusiasm for your cause, business, products, or yourself as a personality is restricted only by the extent to which you are willing to create fierce opposition.

The Largest Public Seminar Company Is Led by Someone Who Offends with Every Speech

Let me give you a fantastic example. My friend and business colleague, Peter Lowe, has built, in five short years, the largest public seminar company in the world. When I started speaking on Peter's programs, it was him, Zig Ziglar, and myself, with two or three thousand people at the events. Today, it is Peter, Zig, me, former President Bush, General Norman Schwarzkopf, Larry King, coach Lou Holtz, Olympian Mary Lou Retton, entrepreneurs like Debbi Fields of Mrs. Fields Cookies, famous attorney Gerry Spence, even Bill Cosby, all on the same programs, speaking to audiences of twenty to thirty thousand people in venues like Key Arena in Seattle, AmericaWest Arena in Phoenix, or the Thunderdome in Tampa. In a year, well over a half-million people attend Peter's events. Now, here's an interesting "wrinkle." Peter is a devout, evangelistic Christian who, at every event, includes a brief presentation about the Bible and biblical success principles, invites attendees to accept free Christian publications and sign up for his Prayer Letter, and he and Zig both directly give testimony to their faith. As you might guess, this offends some people. Some of the attendees complain. Some even demand (and are given) refunds. And the media covering these events often rake Peter over the coals for "springing" a religious "pitch" on an unsuspecting audience. By doing what he does, Peter knows he will offend people, be criticized by people, and be criticized by newspaper, magazine, radio, and TV reporters. Business experts would advise Peter against doing this. But Peter is more than willing to trade off being disliked and criticized by some in order to have life-changing impact on others, and Peter understands that his opportunity and ability to have strong impact is actually linked to his willingness to strongly offend.

You can join the business experts in arguing against the wisdom of Peter's use of these public events marketed to business owners and sales professionals as an opportunity to give testimony to his faith and to urge others to join him. You can argue that. But you canNOT argue with the phenomenal success Peter has had personally and that these events experience in every city, without exception. In every city this event is held a second time, attendance is bigger than it was the first time. In every city this event is held a third time, attendance is bigger than it was the second time. An ever-increasing list of business leaders, celebrated authors, champion athletes, star entertainers, political leaders, and top speakers ask to get on these programs. By any standard you choose to apply, Peter Lowe International's Success Events are, far and away, the biggest, most star-studded, most attended, most successful seminars.

CONTRARIAN SUCCESS STRATEGY:

You cannot afford to be humble. If you wait to be discovered and rewarded based on merit alone, you had better bring a lunch and several good books because you're going to be waiting a long, long time. The bigger your ambitions, the more likely you are to offend people while achieving those ambitions. And your opportunity to have meaningful impact will be in direct proportion to your willingness to offend. What others perceive as arrogance may very well be the level of confidence, self-promotion, and pushiness necessary. Also, arrogance magnetically attracts more than it repels because many people prefer association with an individual who is absolutely certain of himself and his convictions.

A Pox on Creativity

"I have never made the slightest effort to compose anything original."

—Wolfgang Amadeus Mozart

When I decided to get into the advertising business, I had this mental picture of wild-eyed creative people, some smoking that funny weed, in a giant, cluttered, chaotic conference room, shouting out ideas, being creative. It was somewhat of a shock to find out that most effective advertising is not created this way. Actually, the opposite is pretty much true. Some of the smartest, highest paid strategists I now know in advertising, who come up with famous campaigns you see on TV or in your favorite magazine, are very organized, disciplined people who amass and consider huge amounts of data and information and finally arrive at their ideas in a very deliberate fashion.

As I've grown older, however, I've come to appreciate this pedantic approach. And to abhor the "new" or "original" idea.

These days, I want to shoot fish in a barrel. I want it to be a small barrel. No water. A very large fish. And I'd like an Uzi. If that sounds unsportsmanlike, you're right. But it is very pragmatic. Because here's what I discovered down at the bank: When I go in to make a deposit, nobody asks if I made that money by being creative, from original ideas, or not. Nobody seems to care about that. They do not give me a "bonus" of, say, 10 percent or 20 percent if I did make that money by being wildly creative and original and imaginative. They do not assess a penalty and reduce my deposit by, say, 10 percent or 20 percent if I made that money by copying something someone else has already done.

The Incredible Power of Doing the Ordinary Well

A client of mine in Dayton, Ohio, Marty Grunder, started a little business while going to college; he mowed lawns. He started out with one piece of equipment (a lawn mower), one employee (himself), and one simple marketing plan—he would ask people if they wanted their lawns mowed and, if they said yes, he would do an exemplary job, then offer a continuing contract. Last year, his business did well over a million dollars in sales. His company now does everything from the simple mowing of lawns to complex landscaping projects for businesses as well as homes. In the winter, they plow snow out of driveways and parking lots. In a very short period of time, Marty's company has become the biggest and best-known landscaping company in southern Ohio.

And he didn't "create" anything. He studied the customer service and customer satisfaction principles and techniques used by the companies in other businesses with the most loyal customers—like Nordstrom, Sewell Cadillac—and copied those that he could. He insisted that everybody on his team be neatly attired in uniforms, that trucks and equipment be kept clean, that scheduled appointments be honored. He collected newsletters used by other businesses, then put together a similar customer newsletter of his own. Marty is in a very ordinary business. He does not have any superior technology, new inventions, innovative advantages. He is only doing fundamental things very well. And getting rich doing them.

Whenever I talk with people about this, I point out Fred

DeLuca's Subway chain. Is there anything more basic than a sub sandwich? Well, Fred understands the magic of simplicity. While much of the fast food industry wrestles with saturation issues, his franchises are proliferating like burger joints did in the 1950s. He opened his first store in 1965, at age seventeen, with a $1,000 loan. Now the Subway chain is second in number of outlets only to McDonald's, although much younger than McDonald's, and the race is on. And Subway doesn't even have its own "special sauce." Something simple, ordinary, and uncreative: fresh cold cuts and toppings, fresh-baked rolls, convenient locations, and straightforward, product-driven advertising. Nothing here that any of thousands of independent mom-and-pop sub shop owners couldn't have done to turn their tiny businesses into global empires. No creativity required.

Fred, by the way, has taken between $20 and $50 million in personal compensation out of the franchising business each year for the past five years. No creativity required.

Why "Creativity" Won't Make You Rich

In the past couple of years, largely thanks to the publication of my book *How to Make Millions with Your Ideas*, I've been doing more and more work with inventors: speaking to groups of inventors, conversing with them on the phone, and providing services to them through a company I own an interest in, Inventor's Friend, Inc. As you might imagine, inventors are very "into" ideas. They are obsessed with the great idea. Many of them develop ideas and become paranoid about protecting their ideas. They invest thousands of dollars in patents, trademarks, copyrights, and lawyers' bills. As a result, they seem to feel entitled to something magical happening. Some big company discovering them, like a movie producer might discover a future starlet working in a Dairy Queen in Iowa. Somebody taking on all the risk and responsibility and giving them big money to license their idea, then paying them fat royalties forevermore.

It happens. Just not very often.

Most of these inventors wind up broke, discouraged, frustrated, even bitter. Or they get ripped off by con artists who pander to them and their delusional valuing of the idea itself.

As someone who has thousands of inventors, authors, manufacturers, and entrepreneurs bringing me supposedly new ideas and new products every year, I can tell you that ideas truly are a dime a dozen. No creative person likes hearing that, but it is true.

Ideas take on value through development, positioning in the marketplace, sales and marketing to prove potential, and lots of hard work. The majority of the inventors who get rich do so by bringing their ideas to fruition themselves and building businesses around them. A hundred people will have the same innovative and promising idea today, each erroneously believing he or she is alone. As many as ten may get as far as protecting the idea. But only one will do all the mundane, ordinary, very uncreative hard work of raising capital, finding vendors, and developing a business to capitalize on it. Ninety-nine won't. One will.

I am here to tell you that the creative idea is valueless without a whale of uncreative effort. That creativity itself is worthless unless integrated with and supported by an enormous amount of dogged grunt work. There is an old saying: "1 percent inspiration, 99 percent perspiration." It's valid.

If you happen to be the kind of person who births revolutionary breakthrough ideas, you'd better face up to the reality of having to shelve the thinking cap, put on the work clothes, roll up your sleeves, and do a lot of uncreative, unfun work to turn it into something of value. If you are the kind of person who thinks you never have new ideas and haven't got a single creative gene in your DNA, you ought to take comfort in knowing that ideas alone are like unplanted seeds. What you can bring to the table can be much more important. Certainly creativity is not required to create extraordinary business or financial success.

But It Goes Beyond "No Creativity Required"; Creativity Can Even Get in the Way of Success!

Back to me and the advertising business. And the secret of the "swipe file." Although I get paid very large amounts of money to "create" ads, sales letters, and other literature for my clients, I really am not a very creative person—whatever that is—and I do my best to rein in what creative impulses I do have, because clients are much better served by my copying and piecing together already proven "stuff" than by my indulging my creativity. Here's how world-class direct response advertising is REALLY "created": When I get a new client, I first want to get my hands on everything he's done and the results, and everything his competitors have done that they've continued doing long enough you can reasonably conclude it is effective. From this, I want to preserve and recycle the most useful ideas, themes, copy, offers, and NOT throw everything out and "create" anew, just to demonstrate my ingenuity or to feed my ego. Second, I go to my "swipe files." For example, I have files of "great (proven) headlines" divided up by category, for example headlines for consumer offers, headlines for business-to-business offers, headlines emphasizing guarantees, headlines emphasizing new breakthroughs, etc., etc. From these files, I choose several headlines that can work for my client. Then I go to my swipe files of offers. And my swipe files of story copy. And so on. Eventually, I have pieces, like puzzle pieces, that I can put into order and that provide the foundation for an ad or a sales letter. Then I smooth it all out. Make the pieces connect. Change words, phrases, terminology to fit the client's products and customers. I wind up with an ad that has mostly written itself out of "old," used material.

Now, to be 100 percent honest, I've been doing so much of this for so long that I have some very big swipe files stored in my subconscious, and I can often work with those, without actually, physically raiding the file cabinets in the corner. But the process is the same. The method is the same: stitching together already tested, proven, effective material, NOT creating anything from scratch.

Incidentally, I'm NOT suggesting copyright infringement or outright theft of protected intellectual property. Every good copywriter has a "swipe file" and uses that slang term to describe it—but what we mean is borrowing, combining, integrating, and modifying (rather than creating), so that our new whole is sufficiently different from any of the parts so as not to violate any laws or ethical considerations. However, there are very formulaic approaches to good advertising. For example, there's a very famous, no longer copyright-protected headline originally written by John Caples over sixty years ago, "They Laughed When I Sat Down at the Piano—Until I Started to Play." This has been, and should be, much copied over the years. For example, one of my own borrowings: "Everybody Laughed When I Said I'd Never Work for Somebody Else Again—but I Sure Had the Last Laugh. My Story of Financial Freedom Could Become Yours, Too. Here's How." This headline was for a very successful direct-mail campaign I put together for a client selling home-based business information.

Anyway, in the advertising business, I all too often see creativity for creativity's sake being put ahead of the clients' interests or the desire for results. Worshiping at the altar of creativity blinds people to easier, more straightforward, less risky opportunities. Overrating the importance of creativity holds many people back from pursuing opportunity.

Sometimes creativity backfires.

There's a very big, long-established U.S. company I'm not going to name here that had the same famous logo for over fifty years. When a new president came in, he was looking around for things to change—I think to sort of stake out his territory and demonstrate his authority, the way an animal stakes out his territory by urinating on its border. He brought all the internal marketing folks and his ad agency people together and told them the company had to "get with it," get a new, more modern image. After over a million dollars invested in this creative exercise, the old logo was jettisoned and a new logo was introduced. The old one, by the way, clearly identified the company's product. The new one showed only the corporate name in a very fashionable, difficult-to-read type style. Logos were torn down and replaced on hundreds of stores nationwide, catalogs, brochures, and other literature were transformed, and the company launched an advertising campaign doing nothing but advertising the new corporate logo.

The public reacted, well, by at first not reacting at all. It was a "who cares?" for the consumer. Then, as enough time passed to measure change in market share, the new logo proved to be hurting rather than helping sales. After a number of months, the company's wizards gave in and redesigned the new logo to incorporate the old logo. And that half-breed logo has "stuck" for the last handful of years.

A giant, costly, creative exercise launched by whim, rejected by the public.

God Forbid, We Should Do What Works

At a seminar I did on using certain direct response marketing strategies for agent recruiting in the insurance industry, I started out by introducing "models" and asking: Who is already effectively, efficiently, and very successfully recruiting exactly the kind of people you want but can't seem to get? In this case, the answers are, one, the business opportunity/franchise industry, and two, the network or multilevel marketing industry. For the latter, I used the biggest success, Amway Corporation, as the number one "model" to learn from. But one executive from one of the insurance companies was mightily offended by this reference. Comparing her prestigious, professional company to Amway was an insult! This executive couldn't keep ego and emotion, the twin enemies of logic, out of the way for even a few minutes.

In this case, any of tens of thousands of moderately successful Amway distributors, relative amateurs with modest budgets, recruit more high-income, white-collar professionals in a year than this entire giant insurance corporation does in two years, spending ten times the amount per recruit to get the job done. But God forbid we should try to figure out how they do that and what we can borrow from them to reach our desired results!

In my experience, for every marketing challenge, for every entrepreneurial objective, for every personal desire, there is somewhere a successful model that already has plenty of answers available to anybody willing to pay attention.

The Biggest Copycats Work in One of the Most "Creative" Industries of All

In Hollywood, very little money is made from true creativity, but a whole lot of money is made from putting old wine in a new bottle.

Turn on the tube. *The Jetsons* were *The Flintstones* transplanted to outer space. *Star Wars* was all the old westerns transplanted to outer space. *Mork and Mindy* was *My Favorite Martian* recycled. *Alf* was *Mork* recycled. *3rd Rock from the Sun* is *My Favorite Martian*, *Mork*, and *Alf* recycled. The idea for *Miami Vice* was written on the back of a matchbook: "MTV + cops." The new Superman show is a clever combination of the Superman comic book characters, the Spencer Tracy and Katharine Hepburn newspaper reporter movies, a bit of *The Thin Man*, and a bit of the crackling sexual tension of *Moonlighting*. Copying, recycling, combining.

Why risk creating from scratch when there are so many fantastic models to copy from? This is the network or studio CEO's smart question, as he tries to prudently invest partners and stockholders' capital. I suggest it as a very smart question for you, too.

CONTRARIAN SUCCESS STRATEGY:

Forget all about "creativity" as it is commonly perceived and understood. If you feel like you haven't got a creative bone in your body, you can stop worrying about that, because it clearly does not matter. In fact, even creative folks need to fight creativity for creativity's sake and focus instead on doing what has already proven itself, a bit better. Never underestimate the value and power of the ordinary implemented with extraordinary zeal and diligence.

CHAPTER 7

Forget (Almost) Everything You've Ever Been Told About Persistence

"If at first you don't succeed, try, try again. Then quit. There's no use being a damn fool about it."

—W. C. Fields

Persistence is vastly overrated.

You have undoubtedly been lectured to about persistence. *Just keep trying. Try harder.* If you've bought into this, you've probably also suffered a tremendous amount of frustration and guilt. Because of this "persist at all costs" ethic, those who "quit" often equate that with "being a loser" and lug around that guilt and despair everywhere they go.

It's a harmful ethic. We've actually wound up glorifying the virtue of doing things the hard way, even if an easier path is present, and for doing the hardest thing, even when an easier thing would accomplish the same objective. The American Way became the hard way. Presidential candidate Bob Dole said, on leaving the Senate, "I will do it the hard way. I have done everything the hard way. The hard way has been good to me." Not to take anything away from the service Mr. Dole has given this country or his accomplishments, but maybe this hard way thing is why he looks so old, tired, and worn out.

I would like to redirect you to accomplishing your goals in the easiest way possible. I like shortcuts. I favor getting things done the easy way. If you can get the desired result while lying in a hammock under a shade tree, sipping lemonade, and talking on your cellular phone while someone else pursues the same objectives by fighting traffic, dragging an overstuffed briefcase up and down the street, and sitting in waiting rooms watching time tick-tock away, I applaud you.

Oh, don't misunderstand. I abhor sloth. I detest those who want or take something for nothing. I believe in the value of work. I just don't think there's extra gold stars to be had from climbing a mountain when an elevator's waiting nearby.

Proof That Sheer Persistence
Isn't the Answer to All the Questions

The sales manager's most frequent answer to the frustrated salesman is "Make more calls." The parent's answer to the struggling student is "Study harder." But there's a flaw in all this. Once I said to a golf expert, "Maybe I just need to practice more." "Not if you practice THAT swing," he said.

Let me give you a couple examples to demonstrate how most people persist foolishly:

These days I do a lot of work in the television infomercial business—you know, those annoying half-hour programs that sell you spray paint for your bald head, wrinkle creams, and success courses. I've worked with celebrities like Fran Tarkenton, Florence Henderson, fitness guru Covert Bailey, and many more. This is a billion-dollar-a-year, very high-risk, very high-reward business. The typical infomercial requires $70,000 to $250,000 or even more to produce, and that's before buying the first minute of airtime. The success rate is only about one in fifteen. And here's the quirky part: After investing $250,000 in putting an infomercial together, a $10,000 test, over a single weekend, tells its tale. You know right then and there whether or not it is driving enough people to the phones to order the advertised product.

If it is not making the phone ring, spending another $10,000 or, for that matter, a million dollars airing it some more will

NOT change the results. But the way most people view and define "persistence," they would do just that: keep running the same unsuccessful show over and over again, somehow expecting the results to change thanks to sheer persistence. Won't happen.

You Can Whip a Horse Harder, but You Still Can't Make Him Win

As a kid, I grew up around harness racing. A Standardbred, a harness horse, trotter, or pacer, but particularly a pacer, is a complex animal. A pacer has dozens of different types of equipment to possibly help it race better: hobbles set at different lengths, knee boots, ankle boots, head poles, blinders, different bridle bits, and so on. The blacksmith can give it different types of horseshoes, tilt and weight the shoes differently, put extra grips on or take them off. Every one of those variables can alter the horse's performance. So I learned that as soon as you determine the horse is performing unsatisfactorily, you start experimenting. Systematically, you try out one change at a time. Blinders on—then what happens? Blinders off—what happens? Cotton in the ears—what happens? Et cetera.

But this is not how most people persist. They would just keep racing that horse "as is," probably whipping his butt a little harder each time, trying to change the results through sheer persistence. Won't happen.

Most people would want that darned horse to try harder.

But if that horse has the wrong shoes on, it won't matter how hard he tries. Trying harder won't help. Only getting the right shoes can help. (By the way, did you know a racehorse MUST rest one to three days after each race. He literally leaves his heart out there on the track. Tries as hard as he can.) Telling a racehorse to "try harder" is dumb. Finding ways to free up his peak performance is smart.

Attention, managers, coaches, parents: Just telling 'em to try harder is dumb. Finding ways to free up their peak performance is smart. That reminds me of failing geography in high school. Well, I was failing it. But my parents went out and bought me a globe and a book on how to more easily memorize and remember things, like lists. They didn't just yell "study harder!"; they did what they could to make it possible for me to study more effectively. I brought that F up to a C.

Anyway, most people's ideas about persistence are just a step away from watching the "instant replay," hoping your horse that just finished fifth comes in first in the replay.

Is "Sticking to Your Game Plan" an Admirable Trait of a Tough-Minded Leader OR . . .

Coaches lose plenty of games this way. You see them on TV, coming out of the locker room after halftime, their team down by twenty-eight points, their players beat up and befuddled, and the coach growls to the TV commentator: "We're gonna stick to our game plan." *What?!? Haven't you been paying attention? Your game plan ain't working, man! Your guys are getting their butts kicked up and down the field.* "We're gonna stick to our game plan." This is not persistence. This is stupidity. Oh, and the next thing this coach'll say is: "Our guys just have to try harder."

How a Restaurant Owner Persisted, All the Way to Bankruptcy

Some years ago, I had some friends who were slowly, painfully going broke in the restaurant business. When I dropped by to see them, here's how their end of the conversation usually went:

Well, we're at the end of our rope, but we're going to tie a knot in the end and hold on! We're going to tough it out. Winners never quit and quitters never win, you know.

And they did tough it out. They kept showing up every day at the same time, doing the same things, and moving inches closer to bankruptcy. When the time came that they couldn't pay their suppliers with inspirational sayings, they closed the door and slunk away. "When the going gets tough, the tough get going"—in this case, right out of business, right out of town.

How a Salesman Used Persistence to Ruin His Career

I once watched a salesman slowly destroy his career by accumulating, babying, and finally being buried in "maybes." He manipulated every contact and conversation so that the prospect gave him, and kept giving him, "maybe" as his answer. He had a desk drawer full to overflowing with three-by-five cards of "maybes." And he took great pride in his persistent contact with these prospects, month after month after month.

Unfortunately for him, his much prized persistence had no real-world value. The highest income earners in selling move as quickly as possible to get a definite yes *OR* a definite no. Getting a definite no frees them from investing any more time or energy in that prospect and spurs them on to the next. No matter how much sophistication you inject, selling is, above all else, a numbers game. Speed of getting through nos automatically guarantees more yeses.

The salesman who destroyed his career devoutly believed that if he persisted in contacting these prospects again and again and again, he would eventually get business from them through sheer persistence. He believed that his persistence alone would eventually break down whatever resistance the prospects had.

What Thomas Edison Told Napoleon Hill About Persistence

The late Napoleon Hill, author of the famous book *Think and Grow Rich*, visited Thomas Edison in his laboratory. Edison had tried ten thousand times to make electric light work before finally getting it right. Hill asked Edison, "What would you be doing now if your ten thousandth experiment had failed?"

"I would not be standing here talking to you," Edison replied sharply. "I would be locked in my laboratory conducting the next experiment."

This little story is used by lots of motivational speakers as an example of exceptional persistence in action. "Every time you flick on the lights, you can be grateful that Edison was an extraordinarily persistent man," so the story is told. I say: *nuts*. Every time we flick on the lights, we can be grateful that Edison was a scientist who took a solidly scientific approach to invention.

What Napoleon Hill never spelled out, probably assuming people would figure out for themselves, is that Edison did NOT do the same experiment ten thousand times. He did ten thousand *different* experiments. He tested ten thousand different hypotheses, and he *gave up on* each one as rapidly as possible. He was a "quitter" ten thousand times.

The Breakthrough Success Strategy: Forget About Persistence. Think "Testing"

For the past nineteen years, I've worked in direct response advertising and direct marketing. I want to tell you about what I do for a living in some detail so you can pull a breakthrough strategy for yourself out of how I do business.

Consider a full-page direct-response ad, selling some product. You might see such an ad in your daily newspaper, *USA Today*, *National Enquirer*, or a sophisticated business magazine like *Forbes*. To write such an ad for a client, I'm typically paid $8,400 to $12,600 plus usage royalties. I know that sounds like a great deal of money for writing one ad. I won't bore you with all the research, preparation, and experience that goes into the making of that ad and, in part, justifies my fee. But I will tell you that it is rare for such an ad to be a big success the first time out of the gate. Instead, we often have to do some testing to finally get to the most productive version of the ad. Here are just a few of the variables that can be tested in such an ad:

1. One headline against another.
2. Photograph(s) vs. no photograph(s).
3. One photo caption vs. another.
4. One testimonial vs. a different testimonial.
5. One price vs. another.
6. Single payment vs. "two payments of . . ."
7. One bonus vs. another.

Then, with all that testing done, the outcome is, hopefully, an ad that can run repetitively at a profit. We call that a "control." And as soon as a "control" is in place, the work begins on a new ad that may be able to beat the control.

Throughout this entire process, most of the variables tested fail to make any significant difference. Most of the ads tested against the control fail to outperform it.

How often does a skilled, experienced, top pro copywriter develop a winning, lucrative direct response ad? Maybe one out of every four or five attempts. Or worse. My friend and direct response colleague Ted Nicholas has sold over $200 million worth of his self-published books with hundreds of different direct response ads. He'll tell you that he makes one ad work out of every eight he tests.

In my business, we live with failure every day of our lives, and we must exhibit great patience and persistence—but it has to be the right kind of persistence—that applied to testing and giving up on one hypothesis after another.

Practice Makes Perfect—NOT!

You've been told all your life that "practice makes perfect." What a magnificent lie that is.

Earlier I mentioned my golf swing. You should see my natural swing. My picture's posted in golf courses all across the country like criminals' pictures are put up in post offices. Be on the lookout for this guy. With a golf club, he's armed and dangerous. My swing approximates that of a large barn door, clinging to the barn by one rusty hinge, in a windstorm. On my scorecard, there's no place to count strokes. I count hours. It was astutely pointed out to me that if I go out to the driving range and practice that swing, I will only succeed at more deeply embedding that swing into my psyche and muscle memory.

If the salesman who cannot close a sale sits down in front of a mirror for two hours a day and practices, even memorizes his presentation, what will the result be? His ineffective presentation will be more firmly locked in. He will be better than ever at failing to close sales.

No, practice does not make perfect.

But let's take our struggling salesman and teach him a highly effective presentation, including techniques known to close a very high percentage. Then we have him deliver that presentation and we videotape it. Then we play it back, coaching him on what he did well, what he did not do so well, and how he can improve. Then he delivers it again, we videotape again, we coach again. When he finally owns this effective presentation, he practices using it on his own, in his imagination, running and rerunning a vivid "mental movie" of himself delivering the presentation and securing orders. (This "mental movie" technique is borrowed from Psycho-Cybernetics. See page 7.)

Some years ago, we used this kind of practice, video role-play, and so on to help hundreds of doctors of chiropractic improve their reports of findings and other presentations to patients. In some instances, doctors as much as doubled the percentage of new patients accepting their treatment programs. Doctors' incomes as much as doubled from one month to the next. I have used this same method to coach other professional speakers and sales professionals.

Where Did These Erroneous Ideas About Persistence Come From, Anyway?

Much of what is repeatedly taught about persistence traces back to very different times. Times when a person went to school, then served a couple years' apprenticeship under a "master," then ever so slowly worked his way up a vertical ladder in a single career, vocation, or business. Times when a person got a job with a good company, stayed there for forty years, and retired. You got on one track and stayed on that track. Plodding, mostly, not racing. You kept your nose to the grindstone.

You may argue whether it is good, bad, better, or worse, but this is not the way the world works today.

I never saw my father make an easy dollar in his life. I learned "work ethic" from him, for which I'm grateful, because it is useful and, these days, rare. But it is not a panacea. And I also developed a tendency to try and accomplish my goals by outworking everybody else on the planet. Gradually I discovered that pure, unmitigated, dogged persistence has very little real-world value but often has very high real-world cost. I learned that just one tap applied at just the right place, at just the right time, is more powerful than hammering away blindly, clumsily, and stubbornly.

I used to relish challenges. I believed there was virtue in taking on the toughest challenge and proving to myself and others that I could conquer it, that I could withstand massive amounts of pain and stress. I now view all that as stupid. The older I get, the less interested in challenges I am. I want to shoot fish in a barrel. Preferably one big, fat fish in a small, dry barrel, with a bazooka.

Consider this "easy versus hard" scenario:

Tom H. is a new stockbroker. Like all new brokers, he is handed the White Pages telephone directory, a phone, and told to have at it. If he struggles, he's told to make more calls. If he has superhuman persistence to make hundreds of calls a day, absorb massive amounts of rejection, struggle mightily to get a new client, and survive months of starvation, then the other new brokers who started when he started will fall by the wayside, he will gradually gain favor with his superiors, and finally start sharing in better quality leads. But he will be expected to prove his value through dogged, grinding, persistent effort in an antiquated, unrewarding selling environment.

This strikes me as remarkably dumb on everybody's part.

Let's suppose that, for Tom, I devise a nifty little marketing system that is driven by small, inexpensive newspaper ads and simple sales letters, so Tom never again picks up the phone to make a "cold call." Instead he only talks to prospects who have taken the initiative of calling him, have qualified themselves via questions in the letter, and are somewhat predisposed to doing business with him. He is now much more productive and much less subject to burnout. Is Tom any "less of a man" because he takes this easier way?

In the eyes of many, he WOULD be viewed negatively by jealous peers and confused superiors.

Let's take this a step farther. In one of my mail-order businesses last year, we tested—note that word: tested—three different new products and new ad campaigns. One of the three provided instant, terrific results. Another provided mildly encouraging results. The third, very disappointing results.

It so happens that I have the skills and the resources to turn the second one from mediocre to profitable, maybe even to resuscitate the third one. By doing all the things I described earlier that we do in direct response advertising, by testing one variable after another, by fixing, fixing, fixing, I could, eventually, turn either one of those disappointments into profitable campaigns. I might have to invest sizable sums of money. I would be bloodied, bruised, and exhausted. But I could eventually triumph and have a great "war story" to tell.

I didn't do that. I cheerfully threw the two nonperformers right into the trash and forgot all about them as quickly as possible. What I did was zero in on the one that was a standout winner. I gave it all my resources and attention, turned it on "full speed ahead!" And the result was that I made a great deal of easy money.

Does Money Care Whether It Comes to You Easily or Only After Great Difficulty and Mighty Struggle?

When I go to the bank to make a deposit, nobody asks me: Is this easy money or hard-earned money? The bank does not give me a bonus when I deposit hard-earned, hard-fought-for money. The bank does not penalize me for depositing money made easily. The bank doesn't care.

What Is "Quitting"?

"Winners never quit and quitters never win"—right?

Consider the guy who sets out to learn how to play golf, a difficult game at best. He's going to spend a lot of money on equipment, gadgets, gurus, and practice sessions. He's going to chuck some expensive clubs into the pond. He's going to be frustrated a lot. If his objective, his overriding goal really is to become a good golfer, maybe to play with a group of friends, then all that's well and good and necessary, and he is going to need a bundle of persistence to get the job done.

But if his objective is to get some exercise a couple times a week, to drop a few pounds and keep 'em off, and feel better, he might be better off forgetting about golf and taking brisk walks through his neighborhood. If he comes to this realization after a month or two of "fighting" with golf, quits golf, and takes up walking, what does this say about him? Is he a "quitter" with "no persistence"? Or is he just smart? Is he a "winner" or a "loser"?

Setting goals is, generally speaking, a productive thing to do. Certainly, having a vision of where you want to go in life is important. But too often, people get too nitpicky in micro-defining how they'll get there, thus excluding all sorts of great opportunities and sticking themselves with having to summon up huge amounts of persistence to get to a goal the hard way even if an easier path presents itself.

Since I was a kid, one of the things I wanted to do was be a writer. Early on, I got hooked on mystery novels. I admire the work of the late Rex Stout and John McDonald to the very much alive Robert Parker and John Grisham. For a while, I really worked at writing mysteries. I submitted over fifty different mystery stories to the two mystery magazines, *Ellery Queen's* and *Alfred Hitchcock's*, and I have fifty rejection slips to prove it. I guess I could have locked myself in a loft and lived on scraps while I kept writing mysteries, and maybe, thanks to incredible persistence, I would eventually have made one work. But maybe not. I have my doubts. I might very well have spent my whole life driving a cab or clerking in a convenience store just to pay the bills while writing mountains of stories no one would publish.

Fortunately, I think, I did not require myself to succeed at writing mysteries. After what I felt was sufficient testing—there's that word "testing" again—I quit trying and moved on to a different type of writing that proved much easier for me. And I was able to do it without feeling like a failure.

It turns out that I am remarkably prolific and reasonably talented at writing two things: one, nonfiction, how-to books and related products dealing with business and self-improvement topics; and two, direct response advertising copy for ads, sales letters, brochures, catalogs, and TV infomercials. I routinely get fees of $8,400 to $12,600 or more, plus royalties tied to results, to write direct response materials for interesting clients in dozens of different fields, all over the continent. Doing that is making me wealthy. I've also written and had published six books distributed in bookstores (this is the seventh!), as well as a plethora of books, cassettes, courses, and other information products published and marketed by my own companies, licensed and published in several foreign countries, and sold to the tune of millions of dollars. Yes, it took SOME persistence to get this writing career going. But frankly, not much, because I found what was easy for me to do and did that.

Someday I may again try my hand at writing mysteries.

Maybe with twenty years separating the attempts, I'll be better at it. I don't know. But I'll be testing those waters as a financially secure person and a successful, published author, not as a starving artist in a garret.

Quitters Win a Lot

My friend Mark Victor Hansen failed miserably in business. His construction business went bust. He went bankrupt. And he quit the entire industry.

Most people would prefer hearing the inspiring story of how he went back into that business, started over, clawed his way up, and finally succeeded in a big way. If it took his entire life to do it, it'd be a marvelous story of persistence. And there are stories like that. Mark's just isn't one of them.

He quit the industry entirely, turned his back on everything he knew and had studied for (with the famous Buckminster Fuller), on all his experience, and decided to try an entirely different field. He quickly discovered he had a special knack and love for public speaking. He soon found this to be the easiest way he had ever found to make good money. Over time, he developed into one of the leading inspirational speakers. Most recently, his books *Chicken Soup for the Soul* and *A Second Helping of Chicken Soup for the Soul* have both climbed onto and stayed put for months on the *New York Times* best-seller list. Mark has become independently wealthy. But you might call him a quitter.

I have a client and friend, Len Shykind, who has a frame on his wall with over a dozen business cards in it. Each card is from a different business Len tried. Some he failed at and quit. Some he succeeded at but didn't like and quit. He did not "persist" at any of them, although he did persist in ultimately finding and developing a business he did stay with for over a decade that made him a millionaire. (I describe it in my book *How to Make Millions with Your Ideas*.) Len ultimately built a global company with thousands of distributors. He enriched the lives of a great many people because he was a quitter a dozen times.

If you fly over Ada, Michigan, you'll see the giant Amway Corporation complex that now supports hundreds of thousands of distributors and a billion-dollar-a-year business. It exists because two buddies, Rich DeVos and Jay Van Andel, quit a series of businesses and quit the Nutrilite business, angry at that company's management. If you go to Dallas at a certain time each year, you'll see an army thousands strong of women in pink, driving pink Cadillacs and Buicks, attending their annual convention. The Mary Kay cosmetics empire exists because Mary Kay got frustrated with another direct sales company in which she was a distributor and quit.

CONTRARIAN SUCCESS STRATEGY:

Be wary of the "quitter" label. Rethink your ideas about goals, persistence, success, and failure. Focus on "testing." And look for that which is easiest for you to do, that can take you in the direction you want to go.

All the Investment Advice You Can Get May Be Worse Than No Investment Advice at All

"Never invest in anything that eats while you sleep."
—A racehorse owner like me

The pundits, experts, and predictors who gather at investor conferences, write books, appear on *Wall Street Week* and *Moneyline*, and otherwise dispense authoritative advice on investing have been beat by the throwing of darts at the stock market page of *The Wall Street Journal*, and by a group of "little old ladies."

A little group of silver-haired matrons get together on the first Thursday of every month in the basement of the 4th Street Evangelical Lutheran Church in Beardstown, Illinois, but they're not there to play bingo and work on a quilt. This is the Beardstown Ladies Investment Club. They manage a portfolio of twenty-five or so stocks they themselves pick. During the past ten years, their portfolio has earned an average 23 percent per year, outpacing a great many "professionally managed" funds and stock experts. And they've written a book, *The Beardstown Ladies' Common Sense Investment Guide*, which has climbed right up the best-seller list. Of course.

In spite of their success, pundits like Kenneth Fisher, an investment columnist for *Forbes*, says, "The ladies about whom that book was written are all wonderful, I'm sure, but they also flunk all my tests. I would seek advice instead from more publicly seasoned seers."

Such a comment reminds me of Jimmy Carter's mother. After Jimmy had been a distinguished military officer, successful businessman, and President of the United States of America, and Billy was wandering around drunk, urinating in the street, she confessed, "I like Billy the best."

These opinions don't count much. Results do. And, with all due respect to Mr. Fisher and what I'm sure are his impressive credentials, can he produce his own stock investments and show us 23 percent a year?

The fact that this bunch of little old ladies in a small town can kick the butts of all the hotshot, highly credentialed experts who gather at Ruckeyser's feet on PBS or who are oft quoted in *The Wall Street Journal* tells you a lot about contrarian success.

"A Penny Saved Is a Penny Earned"

No, it is not. A penny saved is, of course, subject to income taxes. The interest earned on the penny is subject to capital gains taxes, and possibly estate taxes. And the penny's value is up against inflation's erosion over time. So let's not get carried away here.

I'm told that there is approximately $8 billion in "spare change" in jars, bottles, and dresser drawers in American homes. I'm not sure what this tells us about people and their pennies. Does this mean that they are practicing the penny-saved, penny-earned philosophy? Or does this mean that people place so little value on the little copper doodads that they just let them lie around the house? The one thing I can tell you is that it'll take a whole heck of a lot of pennies to add up to anything. Like a few lifetimes of spare change.

And I can tell you that, in my experience, people who worry over pennies never make any real money. It's one thing to be frugal. Plenty of very successful people are frugal, practical, and abhor waste. But when it is carried to the extreme of obsessing over every little thing, the penny held to the eye can block out an entire world of opportunity. (Try it!)

My mentor used to warn me about wearing a hole in the pants pocket of a $300 suit carrying around pennies and got me into the habit of giving away my spare change whenever I can. If there's a change collection box for a respected charity in a store or restaurant, I'll dump in all my change.

Differences in opinion about such a thing as a penny tells you that managing and investing money is a complicated and confusing task.

How to Break the Rules of Managing Money, Which Brings Us to Contrarian Investors

Contrarian investors are not talked about that much, but they exist—and often prosper.

Philip Anschultz is one of those big-time investors called "crazy" over and over again by experts and friends. But each time he has been called crazy, he's made fools of his critics and millions of dollars for himself. Back in 1984, Anschultz paid $90 million down for a dinky railroad. Four years later, he leveraged that investment into the purchase of another, bigger railroad. At the time, everybody seriously questioned the wisdom of pouring all that capital into a stagnant, antiquated industry with nowhere to go but down. But in August 1995, he sold the whole thing to Union Pacific Corporation for $3.9 billion. That's billions with a "b." He will net nearly $2 billion, pretax of course. Anschultz also routinely invests in real estate in depressed markets others avoid. And he keeps moving up on the lists of America's richest individuals, according to *Forbes* magazine.

Merle and Pat Woolley are also contrarians in the world of real estate, certainly on a smaller scale than Philip Anschultz, but very profitably nonetheless. Imagine someone telling you this: that they are going to get rich by buying single-family homes at 80 percent to 90 percent of asking price, then selling them to people who cannot qualify for any kind of conventional bank financing, who have troubled credit records, and who cannot put up normal down payments, carrying all the financing and risk themselves. Further, that they will get all the capital needed to buy and finance all this real estate from individual investors, guarantee them an interest rate several points higher than prime, and secure them with deeds. What would you say? Experts say: Why on earth would you pay 90 percent of asking price? Why wouldn't you seek out foreclosures, fix-ups, and repossessions that you can buy cheap? And why on earth would you finance people no bank on earth will finance? You must be crazy!

Crazy like foxes. The Woolleys started about five years ago, with a single property and about $1,000 in capital. Today, they and their investors control millions of dollars worth of real estate, they have a monthly income stream of over $10,000, and have helped hundreds of people buy homes who might otherwise have been unable to do so. They run their little business out of a spare bedroom, with one staff person, and an ordinary personal computer. Over a third of the home sellers, home buyers, and investors all come to them as referrals. Most recently, they have begun teaching their "system" to others and replicating their operation throughout the United States. "What we do," Merle says, "defies all conventional logic and everything that all the real estate seminar gurus teach, but it works flawlessly."

Careful investigation of the investment world at any level reveals that the herd is always late and that the most successful investors are often strolling quietly in the opposite direction from the stampede of the moment.

My friend Somers White has a master's degree from Harvard Business School, at one time he was the youngest bank president in America, he is a former Arizona state senator, and is in high demand for lecture and consulting assignments. He told me about one of his consulting clients, a group that manages over $400 million in its investment portfolios. This group is, by overall governing strategy, contrarian. "Most people are obsessed with the here and now," Somers told me, "but these investors focus on that which is out of favor now but will be back in favor in several years. They work a constant cycle of buying 'dogs' and selling them several years later when they are in huge demand. This might be commercial real estate in an area that is currently overbuilt. It might be a commodity. Stocks. But always contrarian."

To Go Boldly Where Others Dare Not Go

Where just about everybody sees only derelict communities, crime, poverty, and devastation, a man by the name of Jose de Jesus Legaspi sees new opportunity. In south Los Angeles, Legaspi is marshaling groups of daring investors to take over and revitalize decrepit shopping centers, insisting that the people who live and work there are underserved by retailers, fast food franchisees, and other merchants. He is part of an immigrant-led entrepreneurial movement finding its way into distressed neighborhoods in a number of major cities. Latinos, Salvadorans, and Asians are taking economically dead urban areas and revitalizing them. Incredibly, a major survey of cities in 1993 listed Compton and Southgate, two south LA communities, in the top twenty of eight hundred urban areas fostering dramatic economic growth. Over the past ten years, the number of Latino-owned businesses in California has grown at three times the rate of Latino population growth.

Our worst inner cities may ultimately be rescued by these immigrant and second-generation immigrant entrepreneurs, while more sophisticated, better financed, better qualified investors and entrepreneurs first scoff, then watch, then wish they'd gotten in on the action.

As I read about all this in *Inc.* magazine (March 1996), I was reminded of how foolish retailing experts thought Sam Walton was early in his game, when he targeted small, secondary cities, ignored by Sears, K mart, and Target for his Wal-Mart stores. Sam said that there was a lot of money to get out there in those small towns. Sam was right.

Can "Plain Vanilla," Dull, Boring Investing Pay Off?

The media likes to focus on flashy investors who invest in sexy things like high-tech products and industries, sports teams and stadiums, high-risk stock offerings, and exciting new products. High-profile investors like Trump, the late Robert Maxwell, the discredited Bruce McNall, are media darlings all. But there are plenty of quiet, unassuming millionaires and billionaires who have gotten rich investing in very dull, mundane businesses. Like billionaire John Kluge. Although he is known on Wall Street for his buying, operating, and selling of television networks and media businesses, one of the long-time cornerstones of his wealth is his collection of over one hundred coin-operated Laundromats.

The eighty-one-year-old Kluge has also been a contrarian investor his entire life. In post–World War II days, he began buying up outdoor billboard advertising companies, even though it was considered by most experts to be a dying business and an endangered one, threatened by those who criticized them as ugly blots on the landscape. By buying up and consolidating small, regional billboard companies, Kluge built the largest billboard operation in America. Next, when network TV appeared to be ringing the death knell for local, independent television stations, Kluge started buying them up. By the early 1980s, his Metromedia company was the largest operator of non-network-affiliate TV and radio stations in America. Eventually Rupert Murdoch bought Metromedia's TV stations to start what is now the Fox Network. By 1995, Kluge had sold all of Metromedia's businesses, netting out about $9 billion. Not bad for a business started by buying up little billboard advertising companies.

Now Kluge is investing in communications enterprises in such unlikely places as Moscow, Budapest, and Bucharest. In the capital city of Latvia, for example, Kluge's company is providing cable television for about nine U.S. dollars a month—and signing up subscribers at the rate of two thousand a month.

As of early 1996, all this is small potatoes. The company is heavily in debt, experimenting with unproven technology, and generating only a few hundred thousand dollars a month in cash flow. Kluge is busily buying, merging, and combining companies around this odd little enterprise. But as nutty as some observers may think this latest Kluge empire-building effort is, history says it'd be dumb to bet against him.

I'd Rather Invest in Reinventing the Old Than Gamble on the New

I've often said that I am just not all that interested in pioneering anything. Pioneers all too often wind up shot so full of arrows they can't hold water. Why gamble on something new when you can much more safely recycle the old?

I like contrarian investing myself. In 1995, I and three partners acquired all the intellectual properties and rights to the materials authored by Dr. Maxwell Maltz, including his thirty-million-copy best-selling self-improvement book, *Psycho-Cybernetics*. Three of the largest publishing and marketing companies in the success education industry turned down this opportunity. Their reasons? Maltz and Psycho-Cybernetics are old hat. An entire generation is ignorant of Psycho-Cybernetics. There are plenty of contemporary authors to build a business around. Why invest in a long-dead author? And so on.

Contrary to their analysis, however, we instantly started a Psycho-Cybernetics renaissance. One publisher, Prentice-Hall, a division of Simon & Schuster, has rereleased two of Dr. Maltz's books and signed our Psycho-Cybernetics Foundation's authors for a new book. An audio book publisher, Audio Renaissance, has rereleased one Maltz product and signed to produce and distribute another one. Marketing has begun for a comprehensive collection of "the best of" Dr. Maltz's works incorporated in a new home study course: "Zero Resistance Living." And three major mail-order firms have signed on to promote the new course. There are niche market versions of these products being produced, too, such as "Zero-Resistance

Practice-Building for Dentists." A business no one wanted will generate over a million dollars in revenue this year, a lot more next year, debt free.

Some of the really big boys in business feel the same way. Take a look at the entertainment industry, where the "old" comic book hero Batman became one of the most valuable movie franchises of the late nineties. And old TV shows like *The Brady Bunch* get the big-screen treatment and produce big profits. You can't help but be impressed with how Pepsi has reinvigorated and revitalized the tired Kentucky Fried Chicken brand. In the infomercial industry, my client, the Guthy-Renker Corporation, would much rather invest in producing a sequel to a successful show than do a new one—which accounts for the fact that there have been five Tony Robbins/Personal Power infomercials, three Victoria Principal skin care infomercials, and two Vanna White Perfect Smile infomercials.

As I'm writing this book, Kraft Foods' executives have been scrounging around in their cupboards and dusting off old brands in search of new opportunities. Most immediately successful: Crystal Light. You may remember it as a drink powder sold in pouches for dieters. It's over ten years old. But mixed with water and packaged in fancy bottles like Evian water, it has been outselling Coca-Cola's heavily advertised Fruitopia in supermarkets. Robert Morrison, CEO of Kraft's North American foods business, says, "Yesterday's businesses can become today's businesses AND tomorrow's businesses if we're smart enough." The 1990s watchword at Kraft is "reinvention."

Want Safety and Security? The Bank May Not Be Your Best Choice After All

Most people don't know it, but there are still people trying to extricate their cash or other assets from the collapsed savings and loans. People DID lose a whole lot of money in those supposedly "safe" institutions. Still, most people stubbornly put their money in banks, at ridiculously low interest rates that often don't even keep up with inflation and taxes.

A friend of mine, Ted Thomas, teaches people how to invest in tax lien certificates. I won't bore you with the details, but I'll cut to the chase: These doohickeys are double secured; they are backed by the governments to whom the taxes are owed AND backed by valuable real estate worth considerably more than the lien amount. Ordinary folks like you and me can go to auctions and to city and county government offices and buy these things pretty much in any denominations we want and get 15 percent, 20 percent, 25 percent, and even 50 percent returns on our invested dollars. While bank CDs are paying (as of this writing) a measly 4 percent to 6 percent, Ted and his students are getting 400 percent more with no more risk, maybe even a tad less.

You won't hear a lot about this particular type of investment, though, because brokers, financial planners, bankers, and insurance companies can't make any money selling them to you—and they pretty much control the flow of information about investing that reaches the consumer.

I have another friend who, for the past five years, has averaged over 20 percent a year interest on his money by investing in viatical settlements. What the heck are those? Essentially, an investor buys the beneficiary rights to the insurance policy of someone dying of a terminal disease, who needs cash now. The policy is bought at a significant discount from its face amount. The policyholder gets money he needs now while he is alive that he cannot get directly from the insurance company. The investor gets a "sure thing" and a very good return on his money. Again, you won't hear a lot about this type of investment in the mainstream media because the insurance companies don't like it, the other "voices" of the financial world can't make money peddling it to you, and some view it as a bit ghoulish. Still it is available, contrarian to the norm, and highly profitable.

There's a whole lot your banker, insurance agent, or family accountant isn't telling you, isn't there?

The Revolution in Real Estate

He was raised in an orphanage until age sixteen. He worked at a series of dead-end jobs while zealously studying real estate, determined to find a way that somebody with no money could "get in the game." In the 1960s, Albert Lowry revolutionized real estate with the publication of the book chronicling his own rise from zero to millionaire: *How You Can Become Financially Independent by Investing in Real Estate*. When I say "revolutionized real estate," I mean it, because Al Lowry was the first entrepreneur to practice and then teach methods of buying real estate with no down payment.

Prior to Lowry, the accepted norm was a 30 percent down payment. This made it virtually impossible for somebody starting out with little cash or assets to quickly create wealth through real estate. But Lowry pioneered "creative financing" and "owner financing" techniques that literally took the bankers out of the picture and opened the doors for gutsy, creative entrepreneurs to buy large numbers of homes in a hurry and profit as landlords; as fix-up artists to damaged homes; through conversion of ordinary tenants to leaseholders with options to buy, paying a premium for that privilege; and so on. It was not uncommon for Lowry's students to acquire a dozen to a hundred properties in a year or two, starting out with little or even no cash invested at all.

As tens of thousands of people flocked to Al Lowry's seminars, he spawned many imitators, including many who improved on his original strategies, made fortunes for themselves, and wrote their own books and created their own seminars, spreading the word. These included people like Robert Allen, author of *Nothing Down*, and Carleton Sheets, who now has the longest running invest-in-real-estate TV infomercial on the air.

Although constant updating is necessary, these methods continue to work for a great many people today. One client of mine, Ron LeGrand, has made a veritable fortune with his "Quick Turn System" for taking control of and "flipping" real estate, typically holding on to a property for less than ninety days. He has thousands of "students" throughout North

America using his methods and making thousands of dollars on each transaction. Merle and Pat Woolley, mentioned elsewhere in this book, adhere more closely to the original Lowry model of buying right and holding on to properties for years, although, in a different way than "nothing down," their methods of buying, financing and reselling these properties is contrarian and revolutionary. Larry Pino's American Real Estate Institute, a division of The Open University, teaches people how to profit from real estate without ever owning any.

All of this remains contrary to the "norm" perpetuated by real estate brokers, bankers, and mortgage companies. And it must frustrate the bejesus out of the hard-working real estate agent who puts in eighty hours a week to make $50,000 or $60,000 all year long to see and know that practitioners of these contrarian methods often make that much in a couple of months, with a lot less work.

Back to Those Beardstown Ladies

With each investing $25 a month, these sixteen women, ages forty-one to eighty-seven, built up a portfolio worth over $60,000 in ten years. In addition, by writing a book about it that has sold over three hundred thousand copies with that number still climbing, they're going to fatten that portfolio total considerably. The occupations of these women are instructive: secretary, homemaker, elementary school principal, retired dental assistant, retired art teacher, retired medical tech, flower shop owner, retired owner of a dry cleaners, hog farmer, retired bank officer, insurance agency employee, retired farmer, bank trust officer, retired bank teller, and a real estate broker.

Only three, it could be argued, have any relevant experience at all. And that'd be a stretch.

These are ordinary people who put their heads together, educated themselves, used their own common sense, and have been consistently successful as stock market investors—embarrassing the experts so badly that many, like the earlier quoted Mr. Fisher, remain in denial.

In just about every category of investment or entrepreneur-ship, the equivalent of the Beardstown Sixteen can be found; someone or some group of someones kicking the behinds of the experts. It is a joy to watch!

CONTRARIAN SUCCESS STRATEGY:

As with just about everything else, the experts are more often wrong than right about where, when, and how to invest your money. As the little old ladies of Beardstown prove, anybody can learn to be their own best adviser—and almost certainly should. The seers of Wall Street are guessing just like the rest of us. Self-reliance is a wonderful thing.

CHAPTER 9

A Few More Success Myths Blown to Bits, in Brief

Some of the devoutly held beliefs about success and failure can be debunked so easily they don't deserve full-length chapters of their own. Here are a few:

"What's Luck Got to Do with It?"

"You've got to place a bet everyday, otherwise you might be walking around lucky and not know it."
  —Character played by Richard Dreyfus in the movie *Let It Ride*

What's luck got to do with it? Maybe a lot. There is, for example, the famous story about Fred Smith at Federal Express, desperate to cover payroll, taking the company's last cash, flying to Vegas, and winning enough on the craps table to keep the company going. Gamblers love that story. Most of my colleagues in the how-to-succeed business hate it.

Everybody in the how-to-succeed business I know and have ever met, read, or heard vehemently denies the possible influence of luck. They must. After all, if you acknowledge that there is "good luck" and "bad luck" completely outside the purview of personal control and self-determination, you open the door to people saying: Heck, why should I worry about setting goals, managing my time, mastering selling skills, and all that other "success stuff" when I might be skyrocketed to the top or destroyed by luck?

I understand the desire of the how-to-succeed merchants to ignore luck altogether. But they're wrong.

There IS such a thing as luck, good and bad. Whatever you wish to call it, however you wish to describe it, there are simple vagaries of fortune. Coincidence.

On October 16, 1995, David Wittig, the former cohead of investment banking at Kidder Peabody, described a "pure luck incident" representative of many I've had and have heard about from others over the years. One evening in 1986, Wittig says he was having dinner at the Manhattan apartment of Marty Siegel, whose indictment for insider trading would come down a few months later. Siegel was trying his best to convince Wittig to leave Kidder and come to Drexel Burnham. Wittig said he looked Marty square in the eye and asked, "Dennis Levine is in trouble, and there are rumors that Ivan Boesky is next. You once told me you talk to Ivan every day. Marty, are you clean?" Siegel assured him he hadn't talked to Boesky in two years. "With that," Wittig said, "the phone rang and the housekeeper came into the room and said, 'Mr. Siegel, Mr. Boesky for you on line one.' " Thus, the lucky David Wittig did not succumb to the Siegel pitch, did not move to Drexel, which later collapsed, and did not follow Siegel to prison. Had the Boesky call not happened at that moment; had it occurred earlier, before the meeting, or later, after Wittig had left, or not at all that day; had Ivan Boesky been too busy to call, his cell phone battery gone dead, his mistress arrived, whatever, Siegel might very well have succeeded at convincing Wittig to come to Drexel. And Wittig might very well have wound up in an adjoining cell. Instead, David Wittig went to Salomon Brothers as a managing director and subsequently retired, at age thirty-nine, a very wealthy man.

How can you call that anything but luck?

My entire career in consulting, writing, and producing TV infomercials, probably about 20 percent or so of my total business in any one given year, exists because of a casual, unplanned, off-the-cuff, oh-by-the-way conversation between Bill Guthy and me at the conclusion of a meeting where I sold Bill the manufacturing portion of an audiocassette company I was running at the time. Our meeting had absolutely nothing to do with his other business: infomercials. But after concluding all our other business, I asked, purely as a courtesy and curiosity, how his *Think and Grow Rich* infomercial was doing. He said its results were slipping—then, on the spur of the moment, asked if I might look at it and come up with any ideas to bring its performance back up. That turned into a ten-year-plus continuing relationship with the Guthy-Renker Corporation AND many other lucrative opportunities and prominence for me in the infomercial industry.

How can you call that anything but luck?

Just the other day, on a flight from Phoenix to Kansas City, my seatmate was a woman, a training consultant from Tucson, with a degree in psychology, experience in the weight loss industry, a solid track record of developing and delivering custom training programs—absolutely ideally qualified for a project I was currently pitching to a client, even though I had no earthly idea who I was going to get to implement the program.

How can you call that anything but luck?

A very popular quote, "The harder I work, the luckier I get," has merit. I believe in it in principle, because I believe in the work ethic in principle; in fact, I have it so ingrained in my subconscious, I have to fight feelings of guilt when good things occur easily, so I believe that good things—including good luck—are awarded to you by virtue of work and clean living. However, there are plenty of examples to the contrary. That British actor, Hugh Grant, who got caught in a parked car getting sexual service from a street hooker, Divine Brown, comes to mind. His acting career soars. She gets a modeling contract and a book deal. Where's the luck-to-virtue link in that?

What DOES seem to stand up is the idea that you can put yourself in positions where you can get lucky. This is a simple idea. Nobody's going to meet the mate of their dreams sitting at home watching *Seinfeld* and petting the cat. You're unlikely to get a promotion at work by staying in your little cubicle, quietly doing your job, and minding your own beeswax. As the lottery promoters squawk, "You can't win if you don't play." I think you can learn the art of constantly putting yourself into situations where good luck can occur. You can even give luck a nudge now and then. If I had kept my nose in my paperwork and not created conversation with the lady next to me on that flight, I would not have found the ideal person for my business project. If I had just completed my deal with Bill Guthy and not expressed curiosity about everything else he was doing, I might never have gotten entrée to the infomercial industry. That's giving good luck a little, helpful nudge.

CONTRARIAN SUCCESS STRATEGY:

Luck exists. Some people are going to get "lucky breaks" whether they deserve them or not, whether you deserved them more than they did, and there's not a thing you can do about all that. It is as random as where raindrops fall. So don't let yourself get eaten up inside with envy or jealousy. Focus, instead, on putting yourself in as many situations and circumstances where good luck can occur as possible. Then you'll get your share.

"Haste Makes Waste"

Tom Seaver: "What time is it?"
Yogi Berra: "You mean now?"

If haste makes waste, you can't prove it by John Elway of the Denver Broncos, one of the greatest artists of the two-minute drill ever. If there are two minutes left in the game, you'd better be beating Denver by more than two touchdowns. That darned Elway can suffer through an entire game of throwing badly timed passes, getting sacked, running desperately to escape the rush, receivers dropping passes, and sluggish efforts from his backs, then suddenly light up the field and elevate everybody's play and beat you by packing more offense into the last two minutes than occurred in the previous fifty-eight. There's also Jim Kelly in Buffalo, lover and master practitioner of the no-huddle, hurry-up offense.

Is this "two-minute drill" phenomenon unique to football? Or even to sports? Not at all.

There are any number of people I know in business who work best and deliver their best work when under enormous time pressure. My friend Gary Halbert is, arguably, one of the smartest, most successful direct marketing strategists and copywriters in the world. But, like the famous fictitious detective Nero Wolfe, who would only work when prodded by a dwindling bank account, his aide-de-camp Archie Goodwin, and extraordinary circumstances (like a corpse arriving on his doorstep or someone machine-gunning all the orchids in his rooftop greenhouse), Gary only rises out of lethargy to do brilliant work in very, very short spurts, only when his own dwindling finances make it absolutely essential, and then only when intrigued by a project and nagged by staff and client alike. He is legendary for both his talent and his reluctance to employ it. I have known him to sit on a project for weeks, dodging, stalling, finding every imaginable excuse to set the work aside for one more day. Finally, though, with no escape route left, with only hours left to deliver on a promise, he will accomplish in minutes what would take most pros in his fields weeks to do.

I confess I am more like this than unlike this.

I tell people I am the hardest working lazy person on the planet. If there is not an almost insurmountable pile of work confronting me, pressing deadlines prodding me, and plenty of pressure to perform driving me, I won't get anything done at all. And I can and do do more quality work in an hour than most people do in a week. I think I could run that two-minute offense.

There Is Only One Speed: Faster

BSG Corporation, a computer services company based in Austin, Texas, is these days running on a very fast track. Its thirty-seven-year-old founder, Steven Papermaster, insists that the only way to outmaneuver giant competitors like EDS (Perot's old company) and Andersen Consulting is to move much faster than they do. Papermaster strives to create a corporate culture that, in his words, "consciously accelerates time" and in which urgency is at the core of everything the company does. He fights the notion that his companywide meetings, held quarterly, are quarterly meetings; they are "annual meetings," because he wants to get through a year's worth of change, progress, and achievement every three months.

Since starting out in 1987 with four people, Papermaster has pushed his company to 50 percent growth every year, year after year, now employing over six hundred, generating $65 million in revenue. He views his CEO role as keeping the pressure on, pushing, and helping people embrace an ever-increasing pace. For him there is only one speed: faster.

Is there waste in this haste? Maybe. Heck, probably. But in many industries and fields these days, a certain amount of haste-based waste must be tolerated in exchange for not being left behind altogether. In many careers, the same pressure exists, thanks in part to corporate downsizing: forcing fewer people to do more work.

And, like it or not, the speed at which we communicate leaves no place to hide, no time to rest, no opportunity to stall. The fax, E-mail, the Internet, the cellular phone, the modem— they have all put us in instant reach of one another, so the pressure to respond RIGHT NOW! has multiplied. Good or bad, this is what it is. So we must get things done faster.

As a small example of this in action, the etiquette of business correspondence has changed. In place of the formally worded, neatly typed letter, a hand-scrawled message on a Post-It note stuck to the sender's letter and faxed back is now appropriate even among *Fortune* 500 top executives. Is this okay? It IS necessary. And the truth is: It gets the job done just as well as the older, much more polite, time-consuming, labor-intensive method. Much of the "new haste" adopted out of necessity meets this test; it may not be as pretty or polite, but it gets the job done just as well.

"Doin' It on the Fly"

There is a marketing technique called dry-testing that is "officially illegal": An ad is run, a sales letter mailed, or a TV commercial aired without the product actually produced and ready to ship, to determine whether or not it can be profitably sold BEFORE it is produced. And although in violation of Federal Trade Commission rules, my experience is that virtually every direct marketer, small or large, dry-tests from time to time. When they win, the mad rush is on to bring the product the rest of the way from idea to reality, often in a matter of weeks. This is just one example of how real business differs from the nice, neat, step-by-step models in the textbooks.

With most of my projects and my clients' projects, we are *simultaneously* in the "planning" and "implementation" stages. And we very often sacrifice perfection, even excellence, in order to get something out there, working, selling, then go back through and fix its flaws, smooth its edges, and clean up the problems. Paul J. Bouchard is a high-wire-act entrepreneur. In February 1995, he was featured in an article in *Inc.* magazine as a result of his remarkable saving of a high-tech product and company. His comments from that experience illustrate the "do it on the fly attitude":

> *It's easy for a small company to fall into the R&D trap of trying to invent the ultimate product. What typically happens at R&D driven companies is, work never gets finished. I've known some who've had a great idea, hunkered down to develop it further, and when they finally stood back up, found that the rest of the world had gone past. The rule is, get out there, learn from it, and then come out with another version.*

And he told his own team: "Freeze this eternal tinkering and make the thing salable NOW. We'll figure out how to make it $25 cheaper and a half inch shorter LATER."

High Achievers and "Rushing Sickness"

If you want to insist that "haste makes waste," you'll be forced to acknowledge that high achievers accept or ignore the waste and make haste anyway. In the book *Profiles of Power and Success,* Dr. Landrum notes that the superachievers studied all were afflicted with a kind of "rushing sickness": They ate, talked, drove, even slept fast. Napoleon graduated from college in half the normal time. Walt Disney went on prolonged, fast-paced working binges broken up by periods of complete collapse, and slept on the couch at his office nearly half his adult life because he resented the time wasted commuting. At age nineteen, Picasso was turning out a new painting each day. He was warned by art dealers that he would ruin the market for his work. (They were wrong.)

Impatience and intolerance for anything impeding their progress characterized every supersuccessful man and woman featured in this extraordinary book, which I recommend highly. As I think about it, the most successful people I've ever worked with—and there have been plenty of them—have exhibited both these characteristics in great abundance.

CONTRARIAN SUCCESS STRATEGY:

Those who are constantly harping at you to slow down and take it easy probably do not understand what makes you tick, what gives you fulfillment in life, or what is necessary to succeed in the environment you operate in. While those with "the rushing sickness" do admittedly pay a price for their achievements, this is also their key to high achievement. Further, success-oriented urgency does not necessarily have to create waste or require sacrifice of quality. Most people work slower than need be.

"Never Mix Business with Pleasure"

"Every pint bottle should contain a quart."
　　　　　　　　　　　　　　　　—Sir Boyle Roche

What kind of advice is *that*? I hear people sagely quoting it, yet here's one that is so obviously, blatantly dumb you have to wonder if they're listening to themselves when they say it.

First of all, if the business you're in or the work you do isn't pleasurable, start on a strategy immediately to get out of there. After all, well over half your waking hours, for at least forty years of your life, are going to be spent working. We get a whole lot of our self-esteem and psychological satisfaction from our work; in fact, we are dependent on it for these things. If you aren't getting these rewards from the way you spend half or more of your waking hours, don't you think you ought to do something about it?

Second, where is it written that "work" and "pleasure" should be mutually exclusive? I guess this goes way back in time in our society when a lot of the jobs were pure industrial drudgery. There's less and less of that these days, and more choices than ever. There are thousands and thousands of different ways to make a living, with or without a "job." Surely there's one that can provide you with both the financial rewards AND the psychological rewards you require. Find it!

I frequently appear as a speaker on the same programs as Larry King—in fact, Larry is often on right before me, and he's a tough act to follow. You probably know Larry from his very popular, nightly TV interview show on CNN, but Larry actually created nationwide syndicated radio. He had the first such program in 1978, started with just 28 stations, built up to 470 affiliates, and stayed on air for sixteen years. I don't think I've ever met anybody who so thoroughly enjoys everything he does. Larry is loving every minute—speaking, doing his show. He goes through every day like a kid turned loose at Toys "R" Us with an American Express Gold Card. And that, I'd contend, is why he has sustained peak success for such a long period of time.

Third, there ARE lots of opportunities to mix business with

pleasure, and I try to take advantage of as many of them as possible, as do most of the successful people I know. Just, for example, because I travel a lot on business and I am on the road nearly half the time, I often have business trip weeks ending up in a great city, where my wife can join me for two or three days. I own racehorses in a few cities—my passion—so I can route stops to see my horses race into my travels easily and frequently. If you have to travel a lot on business as I do, you ought to use that to your benefit. My speaking colleague Zig Ziglar uses his business travel as an opportunity to play great golf courses all over North America—a perk he has most certainly earned. If your current business doesn't give you these kinds of opportunities but you'd like to have them, change your business or change businesses. (Me, I'm more than ready to start staying home more and I'm busy making those kinds of changes in my business.)

Finally, you've got to know—instinctively—that you are much more likely to be effective and successful doing work that gives you pleasure. In horse-racing circles, it's not at all uncommon to find trainers working in their seventies and eighties not because they have to but because they really can't imagine doing anything else—and believe me, they are infinitely better off than those chubby retired folks in their plaid golf shorts here in Sun City, Arizona, hanging around with a bunch of other retired people, pretty much passing time until the end. One night last year, when I was at Northfield Park, a harness racing track in Ohio, a trainer by the name of Earl Bowman and his wife celebrated their sixtieth wedding anniversary. They had two horses racing that night and Earl worked. And I'll betcha he and she had a fantastic evening. This is why, throughout his career, Earl has been a truly outstanding, successful trainer: because he loves the work so much, he'll die doing it if at all possible.

This is the way I think work ought to be. Oh, you might want to cut back as you grow older. I know I want to work less and goof off a lot more in the years ahead. But I do work I'd never want to completely stop doing, and I suppose that's why I'm good at it.

CONTRARIAN SUCCESS STRATEGY:

Blur the line between "work" and "play" as much as you can. Mix business and pleasure at every opportunity.

Maybe the Unabomber Was Right

"There is a certain relief in change, even though it be from bad to worse; as I have found in traveling in a stage-coach, that it is often a comfort to shift one's position and be bruised in a new place."
—Washington Irving, American author (1783–1859)

Yeah, I figured that might get your attention. Remember that crazy cat, the Unabomber, from 1996, and his Manifesto? Well, I'm not here to defend what he did at all. He committed heinous, violent crimes that cannot be justified under any circumstances. However, a lot of people grudgingly admit he just may have had a good point or two about our headlong rush into maximum technology.

One of the most interesting things to me about technology is how much it has accelerated communication but how little it has improved it. I can easily remember when sending out one or two overnight letters in a week via FedEx, Airborne, or whoever was a big deal. Then that became the daily norm. Then that wasn't fast enough. Enter the fax machine, which moved very quickly from being an exotic office machine to something every office and many homes have, and if you don't have a fax number on your business card, you are looked at strangely. Now, you can get incoming calls and even faxes delivered to you on airplanes, en route. And E-mail is threatening to antiquate all of that.

This has sped up the pace of communication enormously. In some respects, it's instant. Certainly, when we are on the "sending" side of all this, we feel like it's instant and are often frustrated when the response isn't. On the "receiving" side, however, we're placed under incredible new pressure. There's no breathing room left.

Many people feel compelled to be constantly accessible via cell phones and faxes, and to respond instantly via fax or E-mail. They give up control over their schedules, they are stampeded into making decisions without sufficient deliberation, and their results suffer. I wonder if there'll be a backlash.

Personally, by the way, I refuse to be sucked into this. I have stubbornly resisted getting a cellular phone. I check faxes no more often than twice a day, start and finish, if in the office or every two days if traveling. I am not on-line so nobody can E-mail me. And I'll be damned if anybody's gonna fax me in an airplane. There is, I contend, a major difference between using technology to your advantage or being abused by technology to your disadvantage.

I also notice technology impeding quality communication in many ways. Not long ago, I was doing some consulting in a big company where the executives were bragging about being able to go for weeks on end without ever actually talking to each other; thanks to their very sophisticated in-house voice mail system, one-button, send-all fax, E-mail, and so on, they could communicate with each other but never talk to each other. I said, "I think you're mistaken. I think you are going for weeks on end sending messages to each other, but I doubt seriously if you are communicating with each other."

I have, on a number of occasions, gotten on airplanes and flown across the country to meet with someone in person when theoretically a phone call, maybe even memos, certainly a videoconference could have been substituted, saving me a considerable amount of time and expense. But there is something about being face-to-face, in a room together, in person that cannot be replicated by any other means. In selling or negotiating, low-tech beats high-tech hands down.

In the speaking business, there is a mad rush to embrace what's called "presentation technology." There are LCD panels and laptop computer gizmos that fit over an ordinary overhead projector to provide colorful graphic "special effects." There are little gadgets you wear on your belt that give you little electric shocks when you have ten minutes, five minutes, and two minutes left. There are all sorts of these things. I've been watching people use these things, and, so far, I hold a rather unpopular opinion: These are crutches being used by weak speakers. When somebody like Gerry Spence or Charlton Heston or Zig Ziglar or Jim Rohn or, immodestly, myself steps to the stage, we do not need a darned thing but our messages, voices, and personalities to mesmerize an audience for sixty minutes or six hours. That's not accidental or a gift of birth, by the way. That's because we work very, very hard at being able to do that. Personally, I'd rather watch and listen to somebody who does that than watch and listen to somebody who has to be propped up and surrounded by a bunch of electronics in order to survive onstage. Guess that's why I prefer Tony Bennett to a music group that needs a million bucks' worth of electronic and computerized enhancements to get through a song. Or why I prefer a "pure" close-up magician, who can confound you with nothing more than a scarf, to Siegfried and Roy or David Copperfield. And I wonder if the opportunity to rely on all this technology invites, encourages, speakers and other performers to be lazy about their craft.

CONTRARIAN SUCCESS STRATEGY:

Avoid seduction by technology. Ask yourself tough questions to determine whether the technology you let into your life is genuinely working for you, to your advantage, or against you, to your disadvantage. Have the courage *not* to use the trendy, popular technology if it is not right for you.

CHAPTER 10

Special Contrarian Advice for Young People—and Useful to Others

"Whatever the majority of people is doing, under any given circumstance, if you do the exact opposite, you will probably never make another mistake as long as you live."

—Earl Nightingale

One of the things I hear a lot from recent college grads is the extraordinary difficulty of finding a job in the field they've chosen and prepared for. But I happen to believe that you can get a very beneficial starting-point job, in any field you wish, in just about any company you choose, from the owner, CEO, or other "top dog" of your choice. Here, exactly, is why and how.

For starters, forget everything you've been told about résumés, your college's placement office, executive placement firms, and interviewing skills. Just being one of this year's herd of graduates sending out résumés and plodding along the traditional, normal path is NOT going to get you abnormal results. If you want to make something dramatic happen fast, you need a contrarian approach.

How I Got My First Job—Even Though I Was Woefully Unqualified

In 1973, as a high school (only) grad, I needed to get to work and I had decided I wanted to start out in "professional selling." I envisioned a nice, new company car (probably because I was driving a $25 clunker), a salary, commissions, and bonuses, suit-and-tie work, and some glamorous travel. I spotted an ad in the *Cleveland Plain Dealer:* The national sales manager for a publishing company was in town for two days only to hire a sales rep to call on all the bookstores, department stores, and other retailers in a five-state area. For me, "publishing" was a magic word because I had ideas of being a writer and a publisher in the future. And the ad said there was a starting salary of $1,600 to $2,000 a month, commissions, bonuses, expenses, and a company car. It was perfect for me. Unfortunately, I wasn't perfect for it. When I went to the interview, the national sales manager politely explained to me that I was NOT what he was looking for at all. First, I was too young. Second, I had no experience. Third, I didn't have a college education. This position would typically be filled by a thirty-five- to forty-year-old man or woman with a college degree and a significant amount of professional selling experience, not some "kid" right out of high school. And he had several such applicants to choose from. I did my best to sell myself, but he was adamant. I just wasn't qualified.

That's when I pulled the rabbit out of the hat. I said, "Look, you haven't had a rep working this area for six months. Going another three months isn't going to kill you. So here's what I suggest you do: Let me work for you for three months for expenses only, no salary, and I'll drive my own car. If, during those three months, I prove myself to you, you hire me for another three months at half salary but full commissions and bonuses and you furnish the car. If, during those three months, I prove myself, then you hire me on the regular basis, with full pay and benefits. I'll earn the job."

And I was hired. I immediately had some problems, too. I had to go work the company's booth at the Chicago Gift Show but I didn't have a credit card or enough cash to make the trip. The car I had would never make it running around over five states, and the most money I had to replace it with was $300. But I was hired.

In short order, without company approval, I sort of re-invented the entire selling process and I achieved some records: biggest turnaround of a troubled territory in company history; more full rack placements to new accounts in a quarter than any other rep; new, major nonbookstore chain accounts; and more. At the end of three months, I was given my car, full salary, full commissions, and bonuses. I stayed with this company for about a year and a half before switching to self-employment.

A Bold, Challenging Statement Gets This Unqualified Guy the Job That Would Make Him Rich

Another story: Bob Edmiston was young, poorly educated, but determined to get ahead in a career in finance. He worked for a bank, for Chrysler, for Ford, but couldn't get moving. He applied for the position of controller with the upstart Jensen automobile company and was rejected. Not well enough educated. Not enough experience. And so on. But a few months later, the owner called, said he didn't like the guy who had been hired, and invited Bob in for an interview. At the end, the owner said, "You're only twenty-seven years old and that's too young to be a controller and you've never done this kind of a job before. Why should I trust you with all this responsibility?"

Bob answered, "I've read that you started making yourself into a millionaire when you were just twenty-eight years old. I'd like a go at it too."

This is exactly the kind of gutsy, straightforward approach that entrepreneurs like and respond to. Any other applicant would have squirmed in his seat, trotted out more information about his past jobs, and struggled to justify himself in the face of such a tough question. And most job applicants are concerned with their starting wage, vacation days, and health care—not becoming a millionaire. By not responding like a typical job applicant in any way, shape, or form, Bob hit the mark. He reminded the entrepreneur interviewing him of his own early struggles and desires. This entrepreneur hired Bob on the spot.

As an aside, Bob Edmiston points out that it's never really the length of experience that counts—it's the intensity. "You can work fifty years filing papers and learn nothing," Bob says, "or you can work six months in an intense situation and learn a tremendous amount." Bob had such an intense experience at Jensen. As you may recall, the high-priced luxury sports car was a bust. The company went bankrupt in just nine months with Bob Edmiston as its chief financial controller.

After the bankruptcy, Bob formed a little company called Jensen Parts and Service, with less than £6,000 of capital, then the equivalent of about $10,000 U.S. dollars. In seventeen years, Bob built that business up to a value of nearly $450 million. Most recently, its main business has been the importing of cars from Korea to England.

How I Hired a Protégé for the Wage of $00,000 a Year

Several years ago, a young lady just graduated from Cornell sent me a long, twelve-page letter. She explained that she and her parents had been in an audience in Rochester, New York, and seen me speak, that they had all been enormously impressed, that she wanted to learn about direct marketing and to learn to do what I did as a marketing consultant and direct response copywriter, and that she was eager to come and work for me for free . . . no pay whatsoever . . . doing anything for a year, if I would let her observe and glean whatever she could from being around me and my operation. Her letter was an outstanding sales presentation, modeled after the techniques and examples I had presented in my speech and in my books and courses sold at that speech. How could you not give this person at least the courtesy of an interview?

Even though I had not been thinking about hiring anybody to do anything, her letter jump-started my interest in having someone around who could function as a personal assistant, researcher, rough draft writer, and "Jane-of-all-tasks."

When I talked with her on the phone, she convinced me that she was serious, sincere, and capable. She got the opportunity she wanted, and she wound up working only for a month without my instituting a low but escalating compensation plan. She was a sponge. She soaked up every ounce of information she could get. Asked a zillion questions. Sat in on my meetings and phone calls. Worked very hard and worked long hours. After about a year, she went on her own and began doing very well right out of the gate. In fact, from her very first consulting arrangement, she was earning between $5,000 and $10,000 a month!

Hopefully, you can see there is a formula here. I'll belabor the obvious. Were I starting out today, knowing what I know now, but with little educational and experiential assets to present, I would target ten supersuccessful entrepreneurs or CEOs of small to medium-sized, growing companies in the industry I passionately wanted to work in. I would thoroughly research their lives, success stories, and companies. I would prepare individual, lengthy letters to each of them, selling myself, and offering to work for free. I'd Federal Express those letters to my targets. Then, if I didn't hear from them in short order, I'd start pursuing them with phone calls, faxes, ideas, anything I could think of, in order to secure interviews. And I will bet you the biggest steak in Texas that within thirty days, I'd be working for one of those ten leaders.

Although I'm a rare bird, I'm not totally alone in dispensing this kind of advice. My friend Ted Nicholas, a self-made millionaire, urges taking a low-level job with a worthwhile company. "Many college graduates and MBAs can't get a job today and one of the big reasons is their unwillingness to take a lower level job which they consider 'beneath' them," Ted says. "That's precisely why immigrants and minorities make up the biggest portion of the new millionaires in the U.S.—they are willing to take any job no matter how humble just for the chance to get started. There are many such examples. Sam

Yeoung, a twenty-three-year-old man originally from China, took an entry-level job at McDonald's one and a half years ago. His pay? Minimum wage. Within six months he was the assistant manager. Then he became the manager. Today he is district manager earning a six-figure income. Next year he will open his own McDonald's. My guess is he'll be a millionaire in less than five years." Then Ted asks: "Do you think a typical American-born college graduate would take such a position? No way! Instead, they might spend months, even years, collecting unemployment."

Ted insists that there are no bad jobs. Any job, done to the very best of your ability, can and will lead to something better. I wholeheartedly agree. In fact, I think it is impossible to do extraordinary work in an ordinary job and not soon be offered greater opportunity.

I've had the pleasure of doing some consulting work for and getting to know comedienne and entrepreneur Joan Rivers. One of the things I most admire about Joan is her repeated willingness to start at the bottom and work her way up to the top. After the suicide-death of her husband and the simultaneous cancellation of her Fox talk show, Joan was a pariah in the entertainment industry. No one wanted anything to do with her. No opportunities were available. Her agent dropped her, her calls to contacts went unreturned. The only open door she could find was an invitation to work as a regular on the nonnetwork, syndicated *New Hollywood Squares* for the pitifully low wage of $500 a week. Most celebrities of her stature would have run from such a thing. Seen it as demeaning. Embarrassing. Career threatening. But Joan went to work. It was the beginning of her climb back to prominence, respect, opportunities, and wealth. Joan says, "Walk through ANY open door." She is right.

A Word About Not Taking No for an Answer

In 1975, I was running my own little ad agency and trying to start a publishing company. I was always alert for opportunities to obtain new clients. I happened across an unusual classified ad in which a "millionaire entrepreneur" sought a "writer" who could "put his thoughts, ideas, success teaching and philosophy into words" for ads as well as books and tapes. In his ad, he mentioned famous success educators that I had studied, like Napoleon Hill, W. Clement Stone, and Earl Nightingale. I wanted to meet this guy. And I wanted this opportunity.

When I called, I was told the position had been filled a week ago. I still asked to speak to this entrepreneur, but I was brushed off. He was too busy and was not available. But I called every day, sometimes twice a day, for two solid weeks. Finally, he invited me in. We subsequently did millions of dollars of business together; he was, in many respects, my best mentor, and without that relationship it is very doubtful that I would be doing what I'm doing today. What would have happened if I had accepted that first brush-off?

Zig Ziglar tells the story of the saleswoman who couldn't hear "No" if it was shouted in her ear but could hear a "Yes" whispered fifty feet away. If you want to fight through the crowd and gain entry to the career field you want, in the company you want, starting out with the attention of top leaders in that company, you need to be deaf to the "no."

I wonder how many job applicants call back fifty times? Or send a new letter every month for twelve months, discussing different reasons why they want to get started in that particular company? I wonder how many applicants are so determined to break into a particular firm that they will continue to try to sell themselves week after week, month after month, for a year or more?

You'll Instantly Have ZERO Competition

The herd of job applicants is plodding through the personnel office, dealing with the human resources folks. You will be the only one talking to the president. The herd of job applicants is "leaving résumés on file." You will be the only one delivering powerful, persuasive sales letters to the top decision maker. The herd never keeps coming back, communicating repeatedly with those who might hire them. You will be the only one not taking no for an answer. Nobody in the herd would dream of working for free for a year. You will have no competition.

CONTRARIAN SUCCESS STRATEGY:

Neither your college diploma nor résumé has even a penny of value, in and of itself. To get going, you must begin. To get ahead, you must begin. You must get a foot in the door and a hand on some rung on the ladder somehow, somewhere, the sooner the better. A key to success is doing even the lowliest, least desirable job better and with greater zeal than anyone has ever seen anybody tackle that job. Learn to stand out from the crowd in every positive way possible, but most of all, in your willingness to roll up your sleeves and do the dirty work.

CHAPTER 11

When a Dog Bites You, Do You Have to Say "Thank You, Nice Doggie"?

"To avoid criticism, do nothing, say nothing, be nothing."
—Elbert Hubbard

If you saw the famous "Soup Nazi" episode of *Seinfeld*, you saw a true antihero of customer service at work. He was only a slight exaggeration from the true, "classic" New York deli owner who freely yells at customers, takes crap from no one, and would rather lose a customer than an argument any day of the week.

In the entire world, Germany has the worst reputation concerning customer service. Writing in *Newsweek* (March 18, 1996), Bill Powell notes that "if in Japan and the United States, the operative slogan is 'the customer is always right,' in Germany it's more like 'shut up and pay.'" Powell tells of an *L.A. Times* correspondent who was expelled from a Berlin perfume shop because she failed to say Guten Morgen to the owner.

Personally, I consistently find the retail store clerks, restaurant personnel, and other service people in Vancouver, Canada, to be among the nicest, friendliest, and most responsive in the world—although Vancouver business owners and residents are always telling me they envy the superior customer service found here in the States. Whether it is fulfilled or not, it is certainly true that the axiom "The customer is always right" is as American as the flag. We teach it and preach it and write one book after another about how to achieve it.

If you have ever worked in retail or in a service business, you have had "The customer is always right" drummed into your head as the ultimate gospel. This means that no matter how unreasonable, irrational, abusive the customer, you must chomp down on your tongue, never argue, and strive to accommodate and pacify.

Herb Kelleher of Southwest Airlines does not agree, and I don't either. "I think one of the biggest betrayals of employees a boss can possibly commit is insisting that the customer is always right," Herb says. "The customer is frequently wrong. In those cases, we have to support our employees. And we try not to cater to those kinds of customers. We write to them and say, 'Fly somebody else. Don't abuse our people.' "

Kelleher's commitment to his people pays off. Most financial analysts point to Southwest Airlines' remarkably good relationship with its employees as one of its key success factors. *Time* magazine once noted: "Critical to success are Southwest's labor union contracts, which permit an easy, largely voluntary cross-utilization of workers. Thus pilots and flight attendants occasionally help clean up planes, ramp workers sell tickets and counter agents unload bags." Herb's willingness to back up an employee in a dispute with an unreasonable customer is one of many "Herb Kelleher legends" that help him sustain such unusually good morale and cooperation with his workforce. Any company's management that automatically and always takes the customer's side could learn something from Southwest.

There Are Some Customers You Are Better Off Without

Now, here's another side of this "customer is always right" issue: You do NOT want all the customers you can get. To many that's a heretical statement. The idea many business owners have is to get *every* customer they possibly can and do everything they can to keep them. My own philosophy is quite different.

First of all, I "fire" customers and clients from time to time when it seems advisable. For example, in our publications and mail-order business, we guarantee customers' satisfaction unconditionally, no questions asked, no strings attached, no hassle, and we mean it. However, when someone returns one product for a refund, buys another, and returns it for a refund, we surmise two things: One, we are unlikely to satisfy this customer in the future, and, two, it is highly probable that this person is ripping us off by copying our printed matter and recorded cassettes. Because of the high costs of handling returns and refunds, such a customer has no value to us. They are a liability, not an asset. So we "blacklist" them. We remove them from all of our mailing lists and if they order via some other stimulus, such as a magazine ad, their name is "flagged" and we refuse their order.

Second, just like Herb Kelleher, I believe you have to back up your own team members when they are right—so I occasionally have to write a customer a letter chastising them and terminating them as a customer. Certainly there are times when our staff or I are "wrong." We fumble the ball. And in those cases, we owe customers apologies and every reasonable effort to make up for the gaffe. But some customers are simply too demanding or difficult to be worth having.

Only you can decide to what extent you want to go to satisfy even extraordinarily difficult customers. But buying into "The customer is always right" idea wholesale, without caveat, just doesn't make sense.

A Customer for Every Business, a Business for Every Customer

Different businesses are better equipped to serve and satisfy certain kinds of customers than others. Regis McKenna, a marketing consultant specializing in high-tech industries and praised by such people as John Sculley and Alvin Toffler, says that "many companies fail to realize WHICH customers they attract is often more important than how many customers they attract."

I've come to appreciate this a great deal. As a consultant, I recognize that my style, temperament, interests, and bluntness work best with entrepreneurial clients and most often clash and fail with big, bureaucratic corporations. Acknowledging that, I exert no effort to secure large corporate clients—and you can count the ones I've worked with in the past five years on the fingers of one hand. I know who my ideal clients is and I am eager to attract such clients but equally eager to repel others. I think every business has a similar opportunity and obligation to be selective in targeting the clientele it can serve best—while avoiding clientele it cannot serve best.

How Motel 6 Leaves the Light On—Only for Some *People*

A company that does an outstanding job of this in all their national advertising is the Motel 6 chain. This is a bare-bones, no-frills, no-services budget motel chain choosing to be the cheapest provider in its category. What's smart about that is that they carefully advertise for people who want that and nothing more. They do not overpromise; in fact, they lower expectations. Motel 6's basic message is a clean, comfortable room and nothing more at half the price of most other chains. One of their most memorable TV commercials shows a solid black screen. Words appear that say, "What the other, higher priced motels' rooms look like when you're asleep," followed by, "What our room looks like when you're asleep." The message is clear: If all you're going to do is crash for the night and move on the next morning, what else do you need and why pay more?

Their two target markets are traveling salesmen and budget-conscious families driving on vacation. They satisfy these customers. They would fail to satisfy many other types of customers, and wisely go out of their way to nicely let those more demanding folks know: This is not the place for you.

By far, radio has proven to be their most successful ad media. Their director of marketing says, "Most of our clientele comes to us through the windshields of their cars. So we decided to talk to these road warriors through their car radios." For over three years (a long time in advertising!), they've stuck with their radio spokesman, Tom Bodett, a carpenter from Anchorage, Alaska, and essayist for National Public Radio. Bodett's rustic, folksy, commonsense tone is perfectly matched to the Motel 6 customer. And his "and we'll leave the light on for you" tag line has become famous.

This is an outstanding example of very deliberately segmenting the available market, matching your message perfectly with a target segment, and talking to that segment in a way that it will like but that you know will be a big turnoff to the other segments.

One of the key strategies I teach in my "Magnetic Marketing" speeches, seminars, and systems is, rather than advertising your product, service, or business, advertise FOR the customers or clients you want. The sooner you determine who your "perfect match customer" is and target that person AND deliberately repel those who do not fit that description, the better.

You see, not only isn't the customer always right, but every customer isn't always right for your business.

Bragging Rights

McKenna also suggests that many businesses can do themselves a favor by targeting influential customers. Securing impressive, influential customers can greatly enhance your company's reputation and credibility. He tells of one computer systems company that secured Citibank as its first customer. *Business Week* magazine wrote an article about them as a result. The word spread. The reference of Citibank had power with every other financial services company. But, as McKenna points out, if their first customer had been a much smaller, little-known bank or insurance firm, it would have taken much longer for the computer firm's "rep" to develop.

Going out of your way to secure and sustain a relationship with key, influential customers per Regis McKenna can be a very smart strategy indeed. I can tell you that having Guthy-Renker Corporation as a continuing client for more than ten years—and being able to brag about it—and having them brag about me—has been worth hundreds of thousands of dollars to me, not including what they've paid me directly. A new business can take a giant leap up in stature, credibility, and ability to command top-end prices by initially targeting and securing a few "name" customers.

While the ideas of picking your customers and, when necessary, terminating customers may seem contrarian to you, they are not new. I love the true story of adman David Ogilvy who, when starting his agency, wrote down a list of the ten companies he most wanted as clients, then doggedly pursued them until, over time, he acquired eight of the ten. As a target marketer, I devoutly believe that you can target, attract, and acquire exactly the kind of customers you want, and even precisely the exact customers you want.

The Annual Purge

I also encourage many of my clients to "purge" their customers lists about once a year. This is a time to take a close, critical look at how valuable your customers are to you and how costly your customers are to serve. Most of the time, whether a dental practice or a mail-order company or an industrial parts provider, a variation of the 80/20 Principle applies; in this case, 80 percent of your net profits come from 20 percent of your customers but 80 percent of your problems and frustrations come from 20 percent of your customers. Hopefully, it's not the same 20 percent. If it isn't, purging the 20 percent who provide the most problems but the least profits is a smart thing to do. I find that such purging creates a vacuum; nature abhors a vacuum; so the vacuum will be filled—and you have the opportunity to fill it with strategically selected better customers.

CONTRARIAN SUCCESS STRATEGY:

The customer is *not* always right. Of course, you should exert reasonable effort to understand a customer's dissatisfaction, respond positively if possible, accommodate if you can, and preserve a valuable relationship if possible. But you also have an obligation to support yourself or your team members when they are right. Also, strategically targeting customers most likely to be satisfied by your combination of products, services, capabilities, and style of doing business, and periodically purging your customer base of those who are not well matched with you, so as to add more who are, will lead to the most profitable business, most productive staff, happiest customers, and greatest peace of mind.

CHAPTER 12

Warning: You Can't Get Rich Quick—or Can You?

"The American economy cannot be revived without someone getting rich—why not me?"

—Rush Limbaugh

All your life, you've been warned against so-called get-rich-quick schemes and against the entire idea of getting rich quick.

What if those warnings have been getting in your way?

An increasing number of people seem to be laughing at those warnings. In 1995, for example, there was an explosion of instant millionaires thanks to the success of IPOs: initial public offerings on the stock market, mostly for high-tech entrepreneurs' ventures. On August 9, 1995, the Internet services and software company Netscape offered its stock to the public for the first time. On August 8, founder James Clark owned shares of questionable value, if of any value, in a company that had never shown a profit. One day later, his shares were worth $566 million. Marc Andreessen, the company's twenty-four-year-old technical whiz, had shares worth $58 million. Jeff Braun, a $15-an-hour employee of a video game distributor went into partnership with Will Wright, an inventor of a computer game rejected by every major company in the field, and for two years they operated their fledgling company out of

Braun's two-bedroom apartment. Eight years later, their company employs about two hundred people and has about $55 million in annual sales. When it went public in May 1994, Braun was suddenly worth 79 million bucks.

Alan Brinkley, professor of history at Columbia University, told *Time*, "I don't think there was ever a period when wealth was created so instantly through the market as it is today."

But going public is NOT the only way to get rich quick, if not overnight.

Ask my client, friend, and now business partner, Jeff Paul. When he first came to my seminar, he was over $100,000 in debt on his credit cards and he and his family were living in his sister's basement. Three months later, he was pulling down $50,000 a month. And after just a year, he was 100 percent out of debt, living in a large new home half paid for, with a big income, money in the bank, investments, and more. In less than three years, a millionaire. All from an unglamorous, disappointingly simple home-based publishing and mail-order business. He's not alone. Consider Brian Kay or Doug and Julie Nielsen or Joe Polish, all three following the same basic business model as Jeff.

Brian Kay had a successful little business helping families find college funding and scholarships. With encouragement from Jeff Paul and myself, he put his methods and sources together in a "package" to sell to financial planners so they could provide this service to their clients and use it as a means of attracting new clients. In 1995, Brian made over a quarter of a million dollars selling these "packages"—and built up considerable continuing income as the provider of the custom, computerized printouts for every planner selling this service nationwide. Doug and Julie Nielsen, brother and sister, had a nifty little discount coupon book publishing business in Omaha, from which they were earning about $50,000 a year. By putting this into "kit" form and selling it to entrepreneurs and to print shop owners nationwide, they established a huge business almost overnight and routinely make in a month what they used to in a year. Joe Polish looks like a rock group roadie and is a "blue-collar guy," a carpet cleaner who developed an outstanding system for getting lots of customers and has spun that into a business providing the system, ads, seminars, software, and a newsletter to carpet cleaners. Starting from scratch, with less than $1,000 put into that business, he generated over $250,000 his first full year, nearly twice that the second, and is on pace to crack a million dollars his third year.

What these three have in common is "quick." In each case, they were profitable by their second month in business and knocking off profits of $10,000 or more per month within six months.

Turn on the TV, Turn on the Money Machine

And don't tell Bill Guthy and Greg Renker that you can't get rich quick. In 1987, Bill Guthy, then thirty-three, running an audiocassette duplicating company mostly serving speakers and seminar companies, and his golfing buddy, Greg Renker, then thirty-one, talked about the enormous volume of cassettes Bill's company was duping for a guy teaching get-rich-in-real-estate seminars via a cable TV "infomercial," a new form of paid advertising. Deciding to jump in and sell something they both believed in, they scraped together, borrowed, and begged $100,000, secured the rights to sell an audiocassette package based on Napoleon Hill's classic book *Think and Grow Rich*, and produced the first "docu-mercial," hosted by Fran Tarkenton, *Think and Grow Rich*. By 1988, that show had grossed $10 million. I was fortunate to get involved then in consulting, writing, and producing for Greg and Bill, helped with sales-boosting revisions to this first show, and I've continued to consult with them as they have built a $200 million-a-year business in less than ten years.

In 1994, media mogul Ron Perelman acquired a 37 percent stake in the Guthy-Renker Corporation, providing a huge influx of capital and financing, priority access to time on Perelman's TV stations, synergy with his New World Entertainment conglomerate, and probable opportunities with other Perelman companies like Revlon and Marvel Comics.

Their business made Greg and Bill millionaires almost overnight. Their business has also made a number of other people very rich, very quick too. The two dentists who invented the "Perfect Smile" tooth-whitening system that Guthy-Renker has sold in infomercials and print advertising featuring vowel-turner Vanna White; motivational guru Tony Robbins, showcased by Guthy-Renker in infomercials with Fran Tarkenton, actor Martin Sheen, and *Entertainment Tonight*'s Leeza Gibbons; the inventor of the "Metwrinch" English-metric tool sets whose self-made infomercial was given massive distribution and his company given badly needed financing by Guthy-Renker Direct; and a number of other entrepreneurs— all owe fame and fortune to Greg Renker and Bill Guthy.

In some respects, Greg and Bill have no choice but to keep "getting rich quick" over and over again and helping others do the same. The infomercial industry is very "hit driven," not unlike the entertainment industry. Trends are important. Predicting consumers' next burning desires is at the core of the business. And having the economic muscle and guts to massively roll out a successful infomercial and its product fast is necessary, because a number of knockoffs quickly follow every success. A new infomercial can go from idea to completed show, on the air, selling products, as quickly as three to six weeks. Most will either prove themselves with over a million dollars in sales in the first month or fail and disappear. In the infomercial industry, "quick" is the norm.

Bill and Greg are not alone. Home shopping channels like QVC and HSN have the awesome power of creating overnight millionaires. I personally know of several people who have gone on one of these channels with their product for the very first time and, in one weekend, gone from nowhere to $250,000, $500,000, or more in sales plus larger, instant commitments for future purchases from the network. Little-known products, like an obscure citrus oil–based spot remover, become household name brands almost instantly thanks to this unique exposure.

As a result, direct response TV is rapidly making "traditional" methods of selling, distribution, and brand building obsolete. A company like Victoria Jackson Cosmetics can be launched from ground zero with an infomercial and, in its first year, rival what it has taken a company like Mary Kay Cosmetics decades to develop. More "Big Green Clean Machines" can be sold in thirty minutes on a home shopping channel than could be sold by a national army of vacuum cleaner salesmen working twenty-four hours a day, seven days a week, in a year! "Perfect Smile" can match Crest in brand-name recognition and shelf sales appeal in just a year.

TV doesn't have a corner on this amazing power, either. Products like Breath Assure and Breathe Right come out of nowhere and become major sellers on store shelves—and make their inventors and manufacturers millionaires in a matter of months thanks to advertising on talk radio stations. A top syndicated radio personality like Rush Limbaugh can "make" a brand—like Snapple or Laredo & Lefty's Salsa—in a matter of months, too.

Contrary to the moral of the tortoise-and-hare fable we were all read, slow and steady will not win every race.

How Does Huizenga Do It? Fast

"Quick" is an inadequate description of the pace Wayne Huizenga set for the growth and expansion of his Blockbuster Video empire. He knew he needed to move fast, to dominate the market so as to discourage a lot of upstart copycat competitors. At the end of 1986, Blockbuster had just nineteen stores. But it had 133 stores by the end of 1987, 415 by the end of 1988, then 1,079 by the end of 1989. For a period of time, a new store was opening every forty-eight hours. Then every twenty-four hours. Then every seventeen hours. This blazing pace put immense pressure on the company's executives, other personnel, finances, other resources, and Huizenga himself. David Letterman joked that you never see a Blockbuster being built. One minute there's no Blockbuster, the next minute there is. But this grueling, fast pace staved off any organized national competition and allowed Blockbuster to achieve dominance in its chosen business category.

When Wayne Huizenga first pulled in an expert and asked him to develop the expansion program, he was told it had taken McDonald's decades to do what he wanted to do in a few years—and that it couldn't be done. But he did it.

Incidentally, Huizenga's plan, as it was designed, then implemented, defied yet another very conventional idea: getting your "fair share." Those two words don't fit into the Huizenga vocabulary. Instead, from the very beginning, he sought total marketplace dominance.

The Secret Power of "Three"

Superagent Ken Kragen, at various times representing the Smothers brothers and Kenny Rogers, and viewed as one of the quietest yet most influential agents and promoters in Hollywood, always tries to create a sequence of three very significant events, one right after the other, in order to make a personality famous. As he points out in his book *Life Is a Contact Sport*, this same strategy applies to making any*thing* famous.

When the Thighmaster was brought to life, three things were hooked together: the very successful direct response TV commercials featuring Suzanne Somers; a blitz of appearances by Suzanne Somers on every morning, daytime, and late-night TV talk show—with her Thighmaster in tow; and, actually, fortunately for them, every stand-up comedian on TV and in comedy clubs making jokes about it. In just a few weeks, the people behind this previously unsuccessful product went from having a dead duck on their hands to having a fortune pouring in.

Why "Slow" Is So Much Harder Than "Fast"

If you'll examine the source of all the warnings you've had against the idea of getting rich quick, you will find that most, if not all, have come to you from well-intentioned people who have not gotten rich at all, at any pace. It is considerably easier to be a sage expert in what not to do than in how to do something. So these warnings must be taken with not a grain but a whole shakerful of salt.

Just about any rich person will tell you that slow is harder than fast, because it is almost impossible to create momentum while moving slowly. A two-by-four across the track will bring a however-many-ton locomotive just starting to move to a grinding halt, while a train moving at full speed'll turn that same board into toothpicks and the passengers probably won't even feel the bump. If possible, you want momentum on your side.

CONTRARIAN SUCCESS STRATEGY:

Why not get rich quick? There's no good reason—only past negative conditioning—prohibiting you from taking a quantum leap. Slow 'n steady does not win every race. Different strategies are best for different opportunities, and often, speed is of the essence and quick is the only way you will get rich with a particular opportunity.

CHAPTER 13

"It Takes Money to Make Money."

"I was the ultimate double threat: broke and inexperienced."
—Hugh Hefner, discussing his start-up of *Playboy* magazine

I suspect more people give up on their entrepreneurial dreams and ideas because of lack of money than any other reason. *I don't have the money to do it. I don't know anybody who does. I can't get the money.* Nuts.

There ARE plenty of experts who will run you through the conventional build-a-business-plan process, forecast two to five years without profit, budget for all manner of equipment and overhead, and calculate that you need somewhere between a zillion and two zillion dollars to start your business. Yet the ranks of entrepreneur-millionaires are chock-full of people who ignored all that, started with next to no money, and somehow clawed and finagled their way to the top. In fact, it is often more harmful than helpful to be sufficiently capitalized and not to have to struggle for survival.

I have long taught: If you can't make money without money, you won't make money with money either. And if you're going to back somebody, pick an entrepreneur who has proven he can survive without adequate capital.

Consider Campus Concepts. In 1995, this company generated

over $4 million. It was started in 1985 for $48. That's not a misprint. Forty-eight bucks. Ian Leopold started his college guidebook publishing business while going to college—where, incidentally, his prof flunked him for his unrealistic business plan. Using other students as commissioned salespeople, Ian rounded up his first advertisers and used their money to finance printing the first guidebook. He gradually expanded the "model" to other colleges, part-time, while getting his MBA and then taking a full-time position with a Cleveland company. He handled the cash flow crunches of growth with his credit cards. "If it weren't for credit cards," Ian says, "I wouldn't be in business." These days, he runs the company full-time, publishing guidebooks for over seventy different colleges in thirty-five cities, with combined circulation of over a million and the support of national advertisers like Sony and IBM in addition to the local advertisers in each market. His original $48 investment has multiplied itself nearly 10,000 percent.

If he had, instead, started out with $50,000 or $100,000 in financing, he would probably have gotten an office right off the bat, furnished it, hired a secretary, maybe hired professional salespeople, extended credit to advertisers, and not been as personally driven to make it pay its own way immediately, day to day. He could very easily have wound up $50,000 in the hole instead of a few million ahead. I've seen it happen many times. Having plenty of money to work with can be a curse.

Even today, when one of my partners in several mail-order businesses start a new one, we loan it only a thousand or two thousand dollars. We insist that it bootstrap the rest of its financing, that it grow with its own income reinvested, not by taking profits away from another of our businesses or cash out of our pockets. Could we afford to make a bigger investment? Easily. Would we do better? I doubt it. Putting this kind of pressure on gets us out of bad or difficult situations quick and early, forces us to make the very best decisions possible, and challenges us to make every penny count. Later in the game we can and do start allocating a certain amount of income every month to off-the-wall experimentation, innovation, failing without worry for purposes of discovering hidden opportunities. But in the beginning we use all of our combined experience and know-how to do only the surest, safest, previously proven things, so that every dollar goes out and gets three more. I think this discipline works. I know it has built a dozen successful businesses for us.

How Ignoring Conventional Wisdom About Costs Created a Record-Breaking Infomercial Success

In 1989, the "buzz" in the infomercial industry was that the ante for quality production was up and up and up, and you could no longer put a successful show in the can for less than $200,000 or so. It was also the buzz that a solo, small entrepreneur couldn't get access to enough good media time to make it worthwhile even doing an infomercial. In other words, either do business with one of the handful of "big boys" or don't do business at all. In the face of this, I produced a show for my client, U.S. Gold, for under $30,000. The company's owner, Len Shykind, made his first tentative, timid, doubtful media buy for a whopping $400. Seeing success, he bootstrapped the income to buy more time. To this day, seven years later, he buys his own time direct from the TV stations and cable networks. And his little, "ugly," cheap show has put millions of dollars in his pocket and more than tripled the value of his company. As of this writing, this infomercial holds the record as THE longest running lead generation infomercial in the business opportunity category. And, incidentally, back at its inception, Len started this multimillion-dollar company with less than $1,000.

Lack of Money Is Just an Excuse

In my book *How to Make Millions with Your Ideas,* I described how Terry Loebbel launched Val-Pak with just $500 in his garage. Nolan Bushnell, who cofounded Atari, the electronic game company forerunner of today's giant computer game industry with $500 and sold it to Warner four years later for $28 million, said that success boils down to just one critical action step: "getting off your ass and doing something."

As I have studied and in many cases met people like Loebbel and Bushnell, who have started businesses with nominal sums of money and built giant corporations as well as personal fortunes, I have become thoroughly convinced that lack of money is just an excuse—and all the sage, expert advice about making certain your business is adequately capitalized is a bunch of hooey.

I have also, incidentally, become convinced that there is no excuse for being unemployed in America. It is too easy and simple to create your own job out of thin air to justify sitting on your duff and living off government handouts. Here are just a few examples of what I mean by creating your own job out of thin air:

A fellow walks between the lanes of creeping and crawling, bumper-to-bumper morning traffic in Boston. He has a very strange device mounted on his back. With much noise and steam, it brews fresh coffee, which he sells to the motorists. He jokes and exchanges stories with his customers, has fun, brightens their days, and makes plenty of money. A "job" created out of thin air.

In New York City, a young woman walks dogs for a living. She reportedly made over $30,000 last year, taking six to twelve dogs at a time for long walks. A "job" created out of thin air.

Another woman recognized a unique need: Businesswomen are constantly running their hose during the day. She started a hosiery delivery business. Customers call her or signal her via her "beeper" and within the hour, they have new hosiery delivered to their desks. Last I heard, this was a $100,000-a-year business.

In the Seattle Airport, you'll find a group of massage therapists have opened a "chair massage center." Weary travelers can sit down, lean forward, rest their heads on padded headrests, and get fifteen-minute invigorating, revitalizing massages between flights. This idea is replicating itself in many other airports.

In a busy downtown parking garage in Toronto, a college student is there Monday, Wednesday, and Friday mornings and, by appointment, will hand wash, wax, vacuum, clean, and "detail" your car right then and there, while you work at your office or go to a meeting, lunch, or shopping.

And here's the newest twist on "selling time" to the time impaired: Lena Shammout, of San Diego, California, charges customers $10 an hour to sit in their homes and wait for the arrival of repair technicians or deliveries. Because most air-conditioning, heating, appliance, and other repair people, carpet installers, furniture delivery folks, and the like will not commit to an appointment time but only to "sometime between ten and four," busy people who cannot stay home all day waiting for them are hiring Lena to do the sitting and waiting for them. How did Lena invent this little business? Out of dire necessity. An eighth-grade dropout and homemaker for thirty years, when Lena went out to get a job, she was asked for her résumé—and she came up blank. At that point, she could have given up. She could have said: Gee, there must be a government agency somewhere to train me for a job or pay for me to go back to school. Or she could have trudged down to the welfare and food stamp office. She started her business with classified ads, bought with the $28 she had in the bank. Later, she traded services to a printer to get flyers she could distribute in her neighborhood door-to-door. Her business has grown, her marketing methods gotten a bit more sophisticated. It's not at all uncommon for her to make $50 to $70 a day as a "professional waiter."

A subscriber to my *No BS Marketing Letter* sent me Lena's story and his plan for creating a bigger business based on the same premise. He intends to advertise the same "lead item," the waiting service, but then upsell add-on services that can be performed while waiting: cooking meals, housecleaning, minor home repairs, and so on. He envisions keeping a large crew of on-call waiters and workers busy, and I think he'll make it happen. If he can keep, say, just twenty people busy, on average five hours a day, at $20 an hour thanks to the combining of services, that's a business grossing $2,000 a week, $8,000 a month, $96,000 a year. If he can then duplicate that in, say, ten communities, he'll build a million-dollar-a-year business. I will encourage him to put it all into a "kit" to sell to entrepreneurs all over the country who want to start similar businesses, and that effort could easily make him a millionaire. And he can start it all with about twenty-eight bucks' worth of classified ads.

Nolan Bushnell's advice is usually the best advice that can be given to just about anybody—the unemployed citizen or the capital deficient entrepreneur: Get off your ass and do something.

As a result of my book *How to Make Millions with Your Ideas,* I did a lot of talk radio shows and took a lot of calls from people with new product ideas. Over half were whining about how they didn't have enough money to get going and needed somebody to invest in their idea or take it, make it happen, and pay them a royalty. The news to be broken to them was never well received. The truth is that ideas, and people with ideas, are a dime a dozen. People with ideas but not enough guts to do anything with them are a dime a thousand. Sure, licensing deals happen. Sure, people invent widgets, license them to some big company, and become millionaires from royalties alone. People win the lottery too. But if you want the odds on your side, you'll get off your butt and go to work turning your idea into a business.

Like Ed Lowe did. Ed died a couple years ago, and that was a great loss, as he was a real character. Ed didn't just start a business; he created the entire "cat litter" industry. He literally stumbled on the idea for gravel-based, absorbent cat box litter in 1947 and, before selling out, built an $85 million-a-year business in a $250 million-a-year industry. From my viewpoint, the humble beginnings of his empire are most instructive. His first product was a five-pound paper bag of the gravel. Its label was his handwriting on the bag with a black grease pencil: "Kitty Litter. Takes the Place of Sand. Absorbs and Deodorizes. Ask Kitty. She Knows."

Lowe got his initial retail distribution by loading up his Chevy with bags, driving around from pet shop to pet shop, doing a little demonstration, and getting each store owner to take a few sacks. He spent several years, as he puts it, "out where the rubber meets the road," securing his distribution one store at a time. He literally cornered the market single-handedly. Largely thanks to Ed, the house cat became America's favorite pet, dethroning the dog from that position. *People* magazine said, "In the history of cats, there are two dates of significance: 1500 B.C., when the little creatures were first given shelter inside Egyptian homes, and 1947, when they finally became proper house guests. That was the year Edward Lowe chanced upon the cat world sensation he called Kitty Litter."

You might argue that such a thing cannot be done today. You'd be wrong. Certainly, you might choose to use a more efficient process than driving from store to store all across the country. But nevertheless, you can start a new product or a new brand from scratch, with virtually no capital and no advertising budget, and make it happen. Consider my client, Rory Fatt at Simple Salmon, Inc., in Vancouver, Canada. I wrote about him in my book *How to Make Millions with Your Ideas* because of his outrageous approach to advertising and marketing his home delivery business featuring ready-to-heat-and-serve gourmet meals. Which he started with less than $500. Today that business is prospering, but he has also birthed a brand for widespread retail distribution. His specialty meals are now distributed by Dairyland Home Delivery to over ten thousand homes AND in 7-Eleven convenience stores throughout western Canada. Rory has built this entire business without benefit of bank financing by juggling credit cards and getting small hunks of expansion financing from happy customers-turned-lenders, obtained by advertising in his own customer newsletter. I even had Rory come and be a guest speaker at one of my $1,500-per-person marketing seminars because he is doing so many savvy things to build his business.

Or consider Neil Balter. He left home at age sixteen before finishing high school and took up odd-job carpentry to support himself while getting through school. While building some shelves in a neighbor's closet in 1978, he got the idea for an entire business based on closet shelves. He began analyzing the "stuff" people put into their closets and figuring out how shelving could be designed and installed to maximize space utilization and flexibility. At age eighteen, in 1980, with $2,000 of capital borrowed from a friend, Neil started his new company—California Closets—out of the back of a van. Neil built that business up quickly as a successful model, then established 150 franchises, and finally, at age thirty-four, sold the whole thing to Williams-Sonoma and walked away a millionaire. After a four-year noncompete term passed, Neil launched a new company, Organizers Direct, this one selling do-it-yourself closet-remodeling kits.

Technology Makes It Easier Than Ever to Start Businesses with Very Little Money

If you use a "broadcast fax" service, you can send a two-page sales letter by fax to any number from a hundred to ten thousand people, all at once, instantly, for about a dime apiece. On a small scale, if you use your own or a borrowed fax machine and sit there and do the manual labor of sending out one fax after another, you can do it in your own local calling area at zero cost. Hard to beat zero cost.

This is how Ron Gorges started his computer repair business for zero dollars. He made up a two-page letter via desktop publishing on his brother's computer. In the letter, he offered to solve any single computer problem for any new client free . . . to come in and teach someone how to use certain software, stop the computer from acting up, show how to get the computer to do something, improve the laser printer copy quality, whatever, any one thing for free. Then he got a list of fax numbers from area offices and companies from a directory he found at the library. Then every night for four hours a night, he laboriously faxed out his letter to one company after another, using his brother's fax machine. Total cost: zero. From four hundred companies he faxed, he got eighteen invitations to come in and solve a problem. From those eighteen, over the next two months, he got over $11,000 in fee-for-service business, one continuing contract at $800 a month, and several good referrals. His business was up and running and making money. With zero investment.

E-mail. The Internet. The ability to run very small, inexpensive ads and use free recorded messages (voice mail) to deliver the rest of the story as opposed to buying big, costly ads. Technology is constantly presenting new opportunities for creating and promoting products, services, and businesses at near-zero cost.

CONTRARIAN SUCCESS STRATEGY:

Stop letting lack of money imprison you. There's abundant evidence all around you that you can turn your ideas into a successful enterprise without having a lot of capital. Access to plenty of money will not "make" a business. Having to fight its way into existence without money will not "kill" a really viable business.

CHAPTER 14

Can It Be That the Product Doesn't Matter All That Much?

"People want things that are hard to find. Things that have romance . . ."

—J. Peterman

After writing my book *How to Make Millions with Your Ideas,* I spoke to more inventors and people with "product ideas" in a year than in my entire previous career span. I talked to thousands of them at speaking engagements, when they called in to radio or TV talk shows, when they wrote me letters, or even sought me out at airports. Most were fiercely, fearfully protective of what they believed to be their new, unique products—although I've yet to have anyone present me such a product. Most were terrified of somebody knocking off their product. And most believed their product would "sell itself" based on being different and better than all other similar products. I call such people *"product obsessed."* Unfortunately, such obsession rarely makes anybody rich.

Here's the contrarian but true approach: It's the story, not the product!

Consider the exodus of Reuben Matteus, a Polish immigrant who made his living peddling the family's homemade ice cream, first from a horse-drawn wagon, later through stores.

Reuben was not the first to wonder whether Americans would pay a premium price for a premium-quality ice cream. But he was the first to grasp that they would NOT respond to such a simple, straightforward story. He figured—correctly—that people would need mystique to justify paying a higher price. He knew he needed a great story with mystique, mystery, glamour, prestige.

Reuben *made up* a foreign-sounding, difficult-to-say name. To give it some credibility, he added a map of Scandinavia to the ice cream carton. So the next time you whip out your wallet for some Häagen-Dazs, remember it has nothing whatsoever to do with Scandinavia. It is actually an ice cream recipe from a Polish immigrant, first produced in the Bronx. Oh, and just for the record, Frusen Glädjé doesn't have anything to do with Sweden or Norway or anything else exotic or foreign either. It's just a made-up brand name to jump on the Häagen-Dazs bandwagon.

Incidentally, Matteus sold Häagen-Dazs to Pillsbury, and the creators of Frusen Glädjé sold out to Kraft. Each walked with tens of millions of dollars for their efforts.

Let Me Destroy Some of Your Illusions

Ever eat Dover sole? Not sole. Not from Dover. A Belgian waffle? Made up in New York. Belgian my eye. Vichyssoise, that terrible cold soup people eat because it's French, served in all the best French restaurants, and, thus, chic. The truth is that Vichyssoise is the name of the native New Yorker who decided to serve it for the first time at the Ritz-Carlton in 1917. It's as French as McDonald's french fries.

Maybe you've seen or purchased the canned Arizona Iced Tea. This brand of iced tea, packaged in oversized cans with funky Southwest designs featuring purple cactuses and teal mountains, is snapping on the heels of Snapple in many market areas and rapidly becoming a top national brand. Everything about its name and packaging would have you believe it has something to do with my home state of Arizona—and after all, if you can quench thirst in our famous "dry" heat, you can quench anybody's thirst anywhere. However, the truth is that this is a very ordinary product: brewed tea with lemon flavoring, conceived, manufactured and sold by three brothers in Brooklyn, New York. Not a cactus within a thousand miles.

If you want a real eye-opener, investigate the skin care and cosmetics industry. The differences between one brand of "glop" and another are minimal. In fact, many skin creams are identical in formulation except for one "top-off" ingredient that sets up its "special story." In one brand, that ingredient might be aloe vera, in another oatmeal, in another sheep placenta, or, for example, in the famous Nancy Kwan Pearl Cream product, crushed pearls. In the case of Pearl Cream, that little extra ingredient IS the story, the ancient Oriental beauty secret of royalty! There isn't a nickel's difference between the actual products, but there are millions of dollars of differences between those with sexy, successful stories and those that fail to ignite the interest of women.

In the infomercial industry, where I do a lot of work, we are constantly besieged by people bringing forward what they devoutly believe are new and one-of-a-kind products, who earnestly believe the product itself should cause us all to drool and cause some company to pony up a ton of money for promotion. They are often offended when they meet a chilly, uninterested reception. The truth is, first, we have already seen and considered dozens of versions of the same product and are just not interested in a product in a vacuum. Instead, what does interest us is the right combination of intriguing and exciting story, dramatic demonstrations, authoritative endorsements, celebrity endorsements, user testimonials, and proprietary terminology. The product is secondary to the combination of these other elements.

Recently, a friend of mine who is really into fishing invented a new kind of fishing rod. His rod has a tube in its center and the fishing line is threaded through the tube, so the line never gets twisted or snagged. He was very excited about this idea. And, although an avid fisherman for many years, he had never seen such a rod. But when he did his patent search, guess what? There wasn't just one or two, there were dozens of these fishing rods with various means of threading the line through the center. Dozens. And not a one on the market. So, because my friend is not just an avid fishing enthusiast but also a very savvy marketer, the other patents are irrelevant to him, and he will proceed with developing a fascinating story about his invention, assembling testimonials, creating a dynamic name, and he will bring his product to market with great odds of success. He understands it's not the product; it's the story.

It's Never the Product—
It's What You Do with It

In my hometown of Phoenix, Arizona, the twenty-seven-year-old founder of Pro-Innovative Concepts has built a $5 million-a-year company with a product that even he admits "is so simple it's funny." It is the Gripp Ball. It's a little squeezable ball that Mark describes as the equivalent of "birdseed in a balloon." Just about everybody thought he was nuts—especially when he started out charging ten bucks for it.

But he has gotten this product recognition as a therapeutic device, to build hand and finger strength for golfers, tennis players, even musicians, as well as for rehab patients and arthritis sufferers. He has popularized it as a stress reliever, successfully sold on the QVC home shopping channel, and imprinted with company logos, as an advertising specialty. His determined, creative, multifaceted promotion turned this dumb little ball into millions of dollars, with no end in sight.

Get this now—we're talking about a darned rubber ball! There is absolutely nothing inherently special about this ball. The only "special thing" is what he has done with it.

Trying to Protect Your Product Is Like Trying to Get a Little Kid to Keep His Clothes Clean for an Hour Before Going to Church

Inventors and entrepreneurs consumed with protecting their ideas aren't likely to get anywhere but into a padded room. The point you eventually get to is that you just CAN'T protect a product itself for very long. Knockoffs are an accepted part of American business. And the speed at which they occur these days is awe-inspiring. In many cases, all a manufacturer must do is very slightly alter his product from yours, and you can flush your patent. If you are eager to protect your opportunities in the marketplace, you do it by protecting your position and your presentation, not just the product. Take my client, the Guthy-Renker Corporation's Perfect Smile tooth-whitening system. As soon as it was apparent this product was a success on TV, knockoffs proliferated at a rabbit-breeding pace. And, frankly, knocking off the product itself wasn't very difficult. But the knockoff artists could NOT duplicate ALL the components that Guthy-Renker had assembled for their position in this market: the "perfect" name; the participation of popular celebrity Vanna White; the use of the infomercial to sell it.

Where to Turn Your Attention, If You Have a Product You Want to Make Successful

The now-famous Breathe Right nose strips, which help stop some people from snoring, present a perfect example of a product doomed to death on the store shelf. There is no argument that this is a marvelous little invention. You'll get no argument from me about the size of the market: the millions of snorers and the millions of suffering spouses. All of the things that would have a product's inventor wildly excited about his product are here, but that and a quarter might get you a cup of coffee. Nothing more. The "magic" here came from the very savvy strategy of shipping case lots of these things to every NFL team and getting the players to try wearing them as a means of getting more oxygen into their lungs and breathing easier in competition. As soon as some pro athletes started wearing them, the TV announcers started talking about them, and— whammo!—people wanted them. The product was nothing without this strategy.

Let's try again. On my last trip to the bookstore, I checked and there are at least two dozen different books about finding your ideal mate languishing on the shelves. But my friend Paul Hartunian sells thousands of copies of his book on this topic per month, probably more than all these titles combined do all year long off the bookstore shelves. How? Well, here's a very important hint: His "secret" is not having a better book than the others. And, incidentally, his has a higher price than most. It is because, each year, he ties a promotion to Valentine's Day, contacts all the radio stations, and offers a "challenge"—that he can take any one of their listeners and guarantee to find them their perfect mate in ninety days or less. He gets booked on hundreds and hundreds of top radio stations as a guest, takes calls, runs these "guaranteed mate contests" with some, and sells books via his own toll-free 800 number. (He's also been on Oprah, Sally, Jenny Jones, and Donahue.) It's NOT the book. First of all, the book could just as easily be a videotape, audiotape, CD-ROM, or aphrodisiac cologne. And his success is unaffected, positively or negatively, by how many other similar products may or may not be out there. His "protection" is all of the components of his "system."

CONTRARIAN SUCCESS STRATEGY:

Comparatively few successful businesses are built or fortunes made because of the true uniqueness and inherent power of the product itself. Worrying about protecting a "unique" product is futile 90 percent of the time, because the uniqueness is an illusion, the protection impractical. Products themselves rarely make people rich. Instead, it is the careful assembly of a collection of product, "story," advertising, marketing, and distribution factors that create a unique and highly lucrative position that can be protected and exploited.

CHAPTER 15

The Illusions of "Marketing"

"Chaos often breeds life, when order breeds habit."
—Henry Adams

Old textbook definitions of marketing, and classic separations of advertising from marketing from sales from distribution, are more restrictive than they are helpful these days.

In too many companies, the marketing departments are bureaucratic enforcers of organizational chart territories and keepers of statistics and research data. In many of these cases, they could be eliminated altogether.

What IS "marketing" all about, today? I believe in "entrepreneurial marketing." Even in big corporations, the true marketers ought to be freed up and encouraged to be entrepreneurs rather than bureaucrats. If you're in charge of marketing, or even involved in marketing, for your product, service, or business, I think you have to constantly question your status quo, your marketing plan, structure, strategies, and beliefs. Marketing is about the discovery of new opportunities. Marketing is about the development of new and better ways to form a stronger relationship with the customer. By my definitions, marketing is an illusion in many businesses. It isn't happening at all!

In this chapter, I've taken a look at two key issues: discovery of new opportunities and new measurements of marketing success.

Controversial economist Joseph Schumpeter defined *entre-preneurship* as "the act of creative destruction." He viewed capitalism as a system that produces material progress through the turmoil and trauma of new technology, new business methods, and new marketing strategies. Certainly there are plenty of instances where deliberately fostering chaos has paid off.

It's worth noting, by the way, that Schumpeter was considered a radical in his time, has since proved to be very wrong about some things and astoundingly accurate about others, and is now viewed by most economists as having been conservative rather than radical. It is interesting how the contrarian often becomes the conventional. Anyway, I buy into the idea that chaos leads to progress, that sometimes shaking things up for the sake of shaking things up is good.

A couple years ago, I spoke at the annual "Excellence in Dentistry Conference," that year held at the Keystone Ski Resort about a two-hour drive outside of Denver. It is a beautiful place, even in summer, when we were there. And I was very impressed with the quality of the staff and the service. It turns out that one of the ways Keystone's leadership keeps their managers' and staff-members' enthusiasm up is the occasional switching of jobs. The ski operations manager runs retail, the ski school director gets to supervise snow making, and so on. Since the rotating managers lack experience, they are forced to rely heavily on staff, so staff members get an opportunity to accept more responsibility and demonstrate greater capability. "Fresh eyes" discover new solutions to nagging problems. Chaos, of course, is an unavoidable by-product. But a very profitable chaos.

I have often suggested this exact same strategy to client-companies of all kinds. Get the top execs out of the ivory tower and onto the sales floor, onto the phones with customers, into the plant. Get the factory folks into interaction with customers. Shuffle everybody around. Let everybody see how the other guy functions. Get people talking to each other who don't normally talk to each other.

Captains of Chaos

Ted Waitt, the founder and CEO of the billion-dollar success Gateway 2000, tossed a big fat wrench into that industry. He turned his back on all conventional means of distribution and turned to direct marketing. By going direct to consumers with a product nobody believed could be sold direct, he was able to cut prices to the bone. And, in what must be terrible heresy to techno-purists in the computer business, he even insists his computer company is not really a computer company at all. "Sales, marketing and distribution is what we're all about," Waitt told *Success* magazine in February 1995. While industry experts laughed, Gateway's sales and profits soared. Currently, they sell over one million PCs a year.

Ted's latest venture: producing and selling a $3,800 personal computer-TV-home theater system, again bypassing all conventional distribution and dealers to sell direct to the consumer.

This willingness to ignore traditional sales and distribution channels has paid off over and over and over again. In my book *How to Make Millions with Your Ideas,* I tell the story of Bob Stupak, who built his Vegas World resort and kept its rooms and casino full by direct-mail selling a prepaid $396 vacation package featuring the amazing benefit of $500 in cash to gamble with. He was widely ridiculed by Vegas traditionalists. They're not laughing now. Vegas World has metamorphed into the Stratosphere Resort, with the giant Stratosphere Tower, now a huge megaresort going head-to-head with Treasure Island, Caesars Palace, and the other biggies.

When Victoria Principal decided to get into the skin care business, to market a signature line featuring the lotions and potions she'd been getting from Aida Thibiant for years, she eschewed any retail distribution, high-end department stores or low-end discount stores, and instead went to my client, the Guthy-Renker Corporation, the infomercial producer. Hollywood insiders predicted disaster. Victoria's career in TV and movies would be destroyed by her selling makeup via a— gulp—late-night infomercial. She'd be a laughingstock. Together, she and the infomercial wizards at Guthy-Renker have sold tens of millions of dollars of Victoria's products, acquired hundreds of thousands of customers, done a series of five consecutive infomercials, and developed one of the largest skin-care products companies in the entire industry. Her entertainment career hasn't suffered either; in fact, the high profile of these infomercials may have helped it. Since the airing of the first infomercial, she has appeared in a number of made-for-TV movies, most produced by her own company, and turned down a couple of offers to star in TV series.

My friends Mark Victor Hansen and Jack Canfield have sold millions of copies of their *Chicken Soup for the Soul* books and built a chicken-soup-for-the-soul empire by NOT relying on the bookstores as their main means of distribution. They've had their books sold—in big numbers—via bagel shops, gourmet coffee shops, chiropractors, and every other imaginable, alternative means of getting a book sold.

They're not the first and won't be the last to sell books outside of bookstores. When E. Lynn Harris self-published his first novel after having it rejected by twelve publishers, his main sales outlets were beauty salons. After managing to move over five thousand copies this way, he was "discovered" by a regular publishing house that signed him for two more books.

In total, if you count "self-published" books, more books are sold through means other than bookstores than are sold through bookstores, and I see no stopping that trend.

Chaos Reigns in Retail

The contrarian approach is permeating the retail franchise industry. Fast food outlets, for example, are cropping up in the most unusual places. It was long believed that the freestanding restaurant was the only way a fast food franchise could be profitable. But today, you can find a Dunkin' Donuts at a racetrack, a Wendy's inside a Wal-Mart store, McDonald's and even Domino's Pizza outlets in airports, and McDonald's is busy opening mini-outlets in Chevron gas stations in fifteen states. Dunkin' Donuts has three thousand outlets in "traditional" locations—most of them, the freestanding store with its own parking lot—but two thousand "alternative" sites. Wendy's even hired an executive away from Taco Bell just to focus on finding more nontraditional sites for their restaurants. He plans to more than double the number of mini-Wendy's in odd-ball locations within the year. Further, what once would have been viewed as franchisee treason is now encouraged to ensure stability and profitability: a single franchise owner combining brands under one roof, in one place. A Sbarro franchisee adds a Häagen-Dazs ice cream and a gourmet coffee unit to his Sears Tower location. In a Las Vegas casino, the same franchisee operates a Subway, a Dunkin' Donuts, and a Pizza Hut side by side.

As they seem to lead the industry in everything, McDonald's leads in this contrarian expansion, too. In 1995, McDonald's launched its biggest-ever domestic building boom, putting the Big Mac in nearly a thousand new locations never imagined before, including Wal-Marts, Home Depot stores, gas stations, airports, sports stadiums, and office complexes. They are also leading the pace in international expansion, with an ambitious target of forty-two thousand more stores to come. Low-overhead "mini-McDonald's" were invented in Singapore. The Dutch invented a "portable McDonald's." Hong Kong, incidentally, is home to over eighty McDonald's, and some of them lead the world in profitability.

Who else will turn their back on the traditional sales and distribution avenues of their industry and make a fortune?

We may see the automobile industry commit to the retail road less traveled very soon. The most respected automotive industry consultant, J. D. Power, told *Fortune* magazine: "Car dealers may go the way of other local retailers in groceries, home appliances, travel and a host of other businesses." He means extinction. Here's why: Already one in ten new-car buyers have found ways of bypassing the distrusted, disliked conventional dealer altogether. They are ordering and buying cars through warehouse clubs like Sam's Club or Price Club, credit unions, affinity buying groups like trade associations, even via mail order or on-line, over the Internet. The number of car dealerships is declining. Major automakers are forcibly consolidating dealerships: Chrysler by 1,500 or so. Mercedes by a couple hundred. GM has budgeted up to $2 billion to shrink its dealer network by 1,500.

The current auto dealer system functions much the same as when Billy Durant invented it and founded Chevrolet in 1911. The new Saturn organization at GM represented the first major change: a tight limit to only three hundred dealers nationwide, preventing cutthroat price competition and virtually eliminating dealer-to-dealer comparison shopping. No forced overinventorying, so dealers can live with a "softer" sales approach. Thus, Saturn has the highest customer satisfaction ratings in the industry. But the next revolution may be to eliminate the salesman and maybe even the dealer altogether. Chrysler and Ford are aggressively researching and quietly experimenting with alternative means of distribution and direct-to-consumer marketing. Ford, which now requires an average of two months to fill a custom order, is committed to cutting that in half by 1999.

Auto dealers have strong franchise contracts, a strong trade association, and a lot of muscle that they have long relied on to maintain the status quo. But little by little, market pressures are driving manufacturers in other, very contrarian directions and, little by little, the dealers' ironfisted grip on distribution is loosening.

Yet another chaotic burp in retailing and service businesses: the twenty-four-hour business day. I quote from *USA Today:* "The time is midnight, but the lights are burning inside the Kinkos copy center. Copy machines are cranking, computer screens invite customers to sign on. Kinkos and its round-the-clock hours is one of the higher profile examples of a growing trend: businesses open all hours to cater to a demanding consumer ... customers who can't find time during what once were considered 'normal business hours.' "

We can throw out the old Rule Book here. Some of the twenty-four-hour marketers named in the *USA Today* article: Al Phillips Dry Cleaners (sixteen stores), Preventive Dental Associates, AutoZone stores, and Fidelity Investments. Here in Phoenix, a mobile auto detailer arrives at his customers' driveways and beautifies their cars between 7:00 P.M. and 7:00 A.M. while they sleep and their cars sit idle. In Boston, an accounting service dispatches its workers to its clients' offices to input computer data from 5:00 P.M. to midnight so as not to disrupt daytime operations. In the infomercial industry, about a third of a billion dollars of merchandise will be sold on TV during dead-of-night and wee-hour-of-the-morning time slots that couldn't be sold to conventional advertisers for pennies. When will we buy a new car at 2:00 A.M.? Maybe soon.

A Whole New Measurement of Business Success

In America, the pressure is on: Corporations are pushed by stockholders, top management, and financial institutions to show bottom-line gains quarter by quarter. This very short-term thinking leads to many decisions that have terrible long-term consequences. In dramatic contrast, Japanese business leaders take a very long view and quietly scoff at our approach. But both use gross sales, market share, profit ratios, and profit improvement, dollars and sense comparisons as the measurement of success.

For years, I have been advocating another, more valid measurement: lifetime customer value, which incorporates retention and repeat business as its key factors. When a business makes maximizing LCV its primary priority, a lot of other economic targets will be hit automatically.

In 1996, in their new book, *The Loyalty Effect: The Hidden Force Behind Growth, Profits and Lasting Value,* consultants Frederick Reichheld and Thomas Teal suggest that customer loyalty is a better predictor of profit and lasting success than is market share, sales numbers, costs, or even the illusive quality of "excellence." They contend—I think correctly—that loyalty most accurately measures marketplace judgment of value and most accurately predicts continuing profit and growth. Their advice, boiled down, is aim for loyalty, not for profits; achieve high levels of loyalty and superior profits are guaranteed. As one of many examples, they point to Lexus automobiles, with the highest repeat customer rate in the entire industry (63 percent). Lexus accounts for only about 2 percent of Toyota's sales but nearly 33 percent of its profits.

This makes so much sense it hurts. Logically, can there be any other standard of success, of excellence, of value provided than the number of customers who choose to patronize a particular company or favor a particular brand, not only repeatedly, but every time, or the majority of time they buy in that category? Yet many businesses, large and small, make no attempt to measure it at all. Some don't understand it at all.

One of the associations I belong to, the National Speakers Association, actually has criteria for its top award designation of "professionalism" that discriminate against the speaker successful in securing multiple bookings from a single client. By their definition, the speaker who is valued so highly by a particular client that that client books him twenty times this year gets to count that as only one engagement, not twenty; the speaker who has twenty different gigs from twenty different clients counts those as twenty. By this math, the "one-trick pony" hired once and only once by each client is twenty times more "professional" than the speaker with considerably more substance and better business acumen who is able to create a long-term relationship with a key client. Unbelievable? Maybe. But uncommon? Not at all. I find that MOST business management is very much concerned with its numbers of NEW customers but completely neglectful of the importance of RETAINED customers.

Just for example, go check out how much the typical automobile dealership spends per sale to sell a car to a customer for the first time versus the amount of money spent communicating with that same customer after the sale, to cement the next sale. It's probably a 5- to 10-to-1 margin in favor of chasing the new customer versus preserving the value of the past customer.

When you measure a business's success in dollars—sales, profits, market share, etc.—you are measuring only what is today with no prediction of tomorrow. But when you measure customer loyalty, you are measuring equity and business value, and that is predictive of tomorrow. If you are going to invest in, say, a hotel chain, which is the more useful set of numbers to know: what its sales and profits were last quarter versus the previous quarter and versus the same quarter last year OR how many guests last quarter were also guests during the previous quarter and during the same quarter last year? Well, the first set of numbers is very subject to aberrant cause and to manipulation. Sales and profits may be up because a competing chain went belly up, a new ad campaign hit just right, a promotion with an airline worked, whatever. But only the second set of numbers reveals the true success of the hotels at satisfying the guests.

The Path to Maximum Profits May Be FEWER New Customers, More Services

I teach small business owners the "mini-conglomerate theory": that it is easier to create and supply more services to the satisfied customers you have than it is to get new customers. One of *Inc.* magazine's five hundred fastest growing companies last year, Capitol Concierge, at five million and growing, was started and is run by Mary Naylor. She lives this idea, continually adding to the variety of services offered to her clients. Of this trend, *Inc.* noted: "Savvy marketers everywhere rue the runaway costs of acquiring new customers. The savviest, one of whom the 32-year-old Naylor has determinedly become, go further. They've responded to these costs and a host of other competitive pressures by focusing not on accumulating more customers but on getting more business from the customers they already have. They aim not to find customers for their products and services but to find products and services for their customers."

In his business of selling how-to information on marketing for financial planners exclusively to financial planners, my client, Jeff Paul, started out with two "courses" in pursuit of every financial planner, then every insurance agent in America. But over a few years, he "creamed" that market, and getting new customers grew increasingly costly. So he grew increasingly prolific at creating and finding additional, specialized books, tapes, software, seminars, and services to offer to his customers. His business's profits shifted from 80 percent from sales to new customers to 80 percent from sale after sale after sale to old customers. And his margins improved.

CONTRARIAN SUCCESS STRATEGY:

Forget all the conventions of marketing, of distribution, of sales. Everything from what normal business hours are supposed to be to where a particular type of product is to be sold to how success in marketing is measured is out the window. The old rules just do not fit the new realities and emerging opportunities. This is the ultimate get-outside-the-box challenge: to erase from your mind how marketing of a particular thing is supposed to be done and start from scratch figuring out how to best reach its likely customers, and to derive greater value from fewer customers.

CHAPTER 16

The Illusions of "Management"

"We have only one person to blame, and that's each other."
—Barry Beck, New York Ranger, who started a
brawl during the NHL play-offs

If you happen to be a stockholder in a major corporation or two, or an investor in many through mutual funds; if you're a regular reader of *Forbes, Business Week,* or *The Wall Street Journal;* if you are attending or recently graduated from Harvard, then you probably have a "vision" of how corporate America's management works. And that vision probably has as little to do with reality as the tabloid articles about Martian abductions of Kansas farm animals.

The Virtues of a Thoughtfully Prepared Business Plan, Sophisticated Market Research, and Expert Analysis—Not!

Here is a wonderful fairy tale about business, especially big business: that corporate leaders are conservative, rational, deliberate people who arrive at important decisions only after carefully weighing a wealth of data and information, input from experts, based on carefully constructed business plans and sound business practices. If you believe this fairy tale, you envision a lot of meetings, where experts provide all sorts of computer printouts and research documents, and pinstriped MBAs from America's top universities engage in logical discussions. You envision men and women of reason operating in a well-organized fashion.

This has *not* been my experience with big business.

Oh, this IS true of many big companies—mostly the ones that are sluggish, that follow rather than lead, fight to preserve the status quo rather than embrace opportunity, and often go from big to extinct before our very eyes. In fact, it is common for a business life to be defined as follows: Stage One, entrepreneurial, quick, daring, and struggling; Stage Two, successful, transitioning from seat-of-the-pants operation to "professional management"; Stage Three, increasingly bureaucratic, slow, sluggish; Stage Four, so bloated, slow, and tired, it rolls over in the night and can't get up, sort of like that sick dinosaur in *Jurassic Park*. In these dinosaurish companies, they live the fairy tale. But usually not for long.

If you expect to achieve great success in or through the big corporate environment, you'll have to bury these ideas.

My experience with really exciting, continually reinvigorated big businesses is that a whole lot of decisions are made in the "ready-fire-aim" entrepreneurial mode. The now-famous story of how Chrysler brought the domestically manufactured convertible back to the street is as good an illustration as any.

As Chrysler began to emerge from its darkest period, Lee Iacocca decided, in his words, that "it was time to start having fun again." He wanted to do something that would be exciting and provocative. One day, a conversation with him and a few workers occurred about how good the LeBaron would look as a convertible. Virtually on impulse, Lee had a crew take a blowtorch to a LeBaron and build a "rough," rolling prototype by hand. He didn't do any focus groups. He didn't employ a high-priced research firm to do a yearlong study on consumer attitudes toward convertibles. He just made one.

Then he drove it around. Everywhere he went, a crowd gathered. "It didn't take a genius to see that this car was creating a lot of excitement," he recalls. "Back at the office we decided to skip the research. Our attitude was: Let's just build it. Even if we don't make any money, it'll be great publicity."

Chrysler sold twenty-three thousand units the very first year, and the convertible has enjoyed enormous new popularity ever since.

Hunches, Guesswork, Gut Instincts, Oh My!

In her book *Pure Instinct: Business' Untapped Resource*, superentrepreneur Kathy Kolbe lamented that "the business world has followed the academic community by distrusting, even demeaning human instinct. Corporations often give more credence to computers than to instinctively based common sense. . . . Many employers demand conformity to a particular method and reject people they fear will act differently. They do this without any proof that a job can be accomplished only one way." She then noted: "Thousands of decision makers in all types of businesses tell me their greatest victories came when they trusted their guts."

In his great book *How the Cadillac Got Its Fins*, author Jack Mingo points out that "the reality is that many of our most beloved products were developed by hunch, guesswork and fanaticism by creators who were eccentric—or even stark raving mad. That's because making something genuinely new requires a different way of looking at things." Creating or reinventing worthwhile products or businesses is more often messy and chaotic instead of organized and deliberate; daring and irrational rather than thoughtful and analytic; based on someone's gut instincts and impulses rather than thorough research; even defying sound business practices rather than adhering to them.

Consider these interesting examples, courtesy of Jack Mingo's research:

The famous Lifesaver candies with the hole in the middle came about by sheer accident and out of a business owner's desperation; stuck with an inventory of defective candies with holes in the middle stamped out by a malfunctioning machine, chocolatier Clarence Crane made the best of a bad situation. However, even after experiencing some success, Crane dumped the business on another man, who pretty much invented the idea of using next-to-the-cash-register counter space for impulse selling of low-priced products, like rolls of Lifesavers. Since the beginning in 1913, nearly fifty billion rolls have been sold. All thanks to accident and invention of marketing ideas by desperation and dire necessity. No careful planning, super business plan, market research, or hard data here. Just a couple entrepreneurs winging it.

"I Am Their Leader. Where Have They Gone?"

How about the Big Mac? Mingo says, "Judging by its popularity, you would think that the Big Mac was the result of sophisticated marketing by a savvy management team. Yet it wasn't that way at all. First of all, it was an idea borrowed from another restaurant chain. And, when it ended up on McDonald's menu in 1968, it wasn't *because* of the company's top management, but *in spite* of it." I especially like the true story of the Big Mac because it demonstrates what I find so common in American business: top management and leadership being dragged and pushed, kicking and screaming, into progress by the rank-and-file troops, not the high-priced, highfalutin' experts they rely on. In fact, I have personally been involved in just that in the insurance industry in the past two years. A fellow by the name of Jeff Paul and I have been revolutionizing the way insurance agents secure new clients, and a lady by the name of Pamela Yellen and I have been revolutionizing the way insurance corporations and their general agents recruit new agents. Gradually, grudgingly, a number of the biggest companies in the industry have come around to accepting and using our dramatically different methods. But only after their ground troops have done all the pioneering, in some cases in secret, hiding it from the corporate folks; only after the ground troops have inarguably proven that this new approach is far superior to the industry norms and traditions. And then still, warily, cautiously, slowly and, in some cases, resentfully. From 1994 to the year 2000, all of the marketing practices of the insurance industry will undergo a massive, dramatic revolution and reinvention, with little thanks to the so-called leaders.

Anyway, one McDonald's franchisee of some influence tested a double-decker burger with special sauce—borrowed unabashedly from "the Big Boy"—in his store, with Ray Kroc in strong opposition. And he had to sneak around behind Kroc's back to get "unauthorized" buns from "unauthorized" vendors in order to make the product work. The much-opposed and reviled new product caused the store's sales to jump by 12 percent. When rolled out it increased companywide sales by 10 percent instantly, and, of course, the Big Mac has stayed with McDonald's and us as a "staple." More significantly, its success opened the floodgates of franchisee experimentation and innovation, leading to the deep-fried apple pies, the "Large Fries," and the Egg McMuffin. If it had been left to corporate leadership, none of these successful products would have happened.

In his later years, Ray Kroc came around to supporting and even celebrating this "from the ground up" inventionism. He was even quoted as saying, "We have to invent faster than our competitors can copy—and we need all the minds we can get access to do that, be that a fry cook or a corporate executive." But early on, Kroc was a very big, stubborn obstacle to change.

How Sneaking Around Behind Management's Back Makes American Business Work

When he was a young officer in the army, Napoleon wrote in a letter to his brother, "I have never paid the slightest attention to the plans sent to me by the Directoire." Napoleon rose to the top following the grand but little mentioned tradition of ignoring the commands of those at the top!

If you've followed Tom Peters's work, you know all about his celebration of "skunk works," groups of renegades inside companies who sneak around and make revolutionary things happen.

Let me tell you a brief but telling story from my salesman days. The chief buyer for all the book departments of a chain of department stores agreed with me that placing large spinner racks of my company's humor and gift books near the front of their departments during the Christmas season would be a huge success—but her company had strict policies prohibiting the purchase or use of display racks, the purchase of predetermined assortments of merchandise, and adding new vendor codes between October and January, except for very small quantity purchases.

She and I spent a very long night writing up individual invoices for each of a hundred titles from the standard inventory packages. We dated the invoices over a period of two weeks, to bring each day's purchase in below the minimum. She found an old vendor's number no longer being used to assign to my company. And we wrote up the rack orders as free and padded the cost into the book orders. I then personally had to walk these weird orders through the bureaucracy at the other end, at my employer's. We circumvented a dozen different corporate policies to get those racks into those stores. The result was a record for dollar per square foot in those departments and the buyer being wooed and hired away by a bigger company.

It is a damned shame that she had to go to such extraordinary measures, to violate corporate policy, in order to do what she knew was right. But this sort of thing goes on every day in almost every sizable corporation: smart people having to lie, cheat, connive, and circumvent dumb policies.

Journalist-turned-manager Bob Woodward told *Esquire* magazine: "All good work is done in defiance of management."

A few companies try to encourage this kind of renegadism and individualism. At PepsiCo, D. Wayne Calloway kept pushing the envelope of decentralization, encouraging individuals to try out their ideas. As a result, there are great success stories. The seventeen-year-old worker in a KFC in Oklahoma City who put his own handmade signs advertising their virtually secret catering service in his store's windows—and increased the catering revenue by 700 percent. Or Calloway's favorite: the manager of the Pizza Hut in Moscow—yes, Moscow!—who sent 150 free pizzas and twenty cases of Pepsi to Boris Yeltsin during the 1991 coup attempt. "That manager didn't call anybody to ask permission," Calloway brags, "he just did it." Calloway is also legendary for his tolerance with the inevitable mistakes that arise from such freedom. But this attitude is very rare in big business. It works, but it is still rare. It is far more common to find employees having to sneak around behind management's backs to do what seems right.

Right this minute, I am in the middle of a most interesting exercise. A group of the biggest franchisees of a large, $8 billion corporation came to us, behind their corporate leadership's back, asking for help. Their sales were off by 20 percent to 30 percent. Competition was getting tougher by the minute. And top management seemed frozen in its tracks like a deer paralyzed by blinding headlights. So the franchisees needed us to provide a dramatically different, exciting plan of action. To get to that point, they revealed all sorts of confidential, inside information to us we would never have obtained from the corporation's executives. This allowed us to perfectly tailor a plan and a presentation to the true situation. Then they persuaded the company's CEO to meet with us. It appears that we are going to proceed with the pilot project that just may turn this entire company's fortunes around. But none of this would have happened were it not for the "underground" actions of a few mutinous but clever key franchisees sneaking around behind the parent corporation's back.

The Virtue of Fair and Just Leadership—Not!!!

In Nashville last year, I appeared on a program with Jimmy Johnson, two-time Super Bowl–winning coach of the Dallas Cowboys, broadcaster and Miami restaurateur, now returned to the sidelines at Miami. In the shortest period of time in NFL history, Jimmy took the Cowboys from the cellar to the Super

Bowl, from disgrace to triumph, from hard times to the very best of times. Anybody who can take a bunch of overpaid pro athletes, some prima donnas, some difficult troublemakers, some hard workers but terribly discouraged, and mold all that into a team of winners—and I do mean TEAM, because the Johnson-coached Cowboys functioned as a well-oiled football machine—knows something real about management. He told that audience in Nashville the idea that a leader should be eminently fair and even-handed, the idea of managing everybody the same way is, in Jimmy's vernacular, "bull."

Coach Johnson says that you have to manage everybody differently. In fact, Coach Johnson says you have to discriminate, to forget fairness and concentrate on results. Management theorists may consider this heretical. Battlefield leaders will instantly recognize it as the rarely enunciated truth.

Here's how it works: Jimmy said he had an informal "scale" for the organization. Those people who showed up on time for meetings, practices, and other events, worked hard, kept themselves in peak condition, studied films and game plans, and adhered to the other requirements of the organization were high on the scale, say 9 or 10. Those who were sometimes late for meetings, had to be pushed to work and were sometimes lazy, who let their weight creep up, who didn't adhere to all the requirements of the organization, were low on the scale, say 2, 3, or 4. Jimmy said the people high on the scale had a lot more leeway for occasional, aberrant errors or screwups than did those low on the scale. For example, a second-stringer low on the scale fumbles the ball. When he comes back to the sidelines, Jimmy grabs him and says, "You've gotta hang on to the ball—or we aren't going to hang on to you." But if Emmitt Smith fumbles, when he comes over to the sideline, Jimmy grabs him and says, "Forget that just happened. We'll get it back and you'll carry it in for the next touchdown. Get a Gatorade." Is this fair? No. Is this right? Yes. Why? Because Emmitt outworks just about everybody on the team. Emmitt is a superstar but not a prima donna. Emmitt is up early, at work late. Emmitt studies and prepares. Emmitt gives 110 percent every time he gets his hands on the ball. The other guy grumbles about putting extra time in in the weight room or gets caught not paying attention at team meetings. Emmitt's fumble is an aberration. The other guy's fumble is a predictable part of a pattern of low-quality behavior.

. Jimmy told the Nashville audience about a player low on the scale dozing off and sleeping during a team meeting. When he woke up, he was cut from the team. But Jimmy freely admitted that if any of a number of other players dozed off in a meeting, he'd walk by, quietly shake their shoulders, and whisper, "Wake up, man." Fair? No. Results oriented? You bet.

Quite frankly, my management experience has been very deliberately limited. I prefer NOT having employees or associates, for a whole host of reasons, ranging from the grudgingly practical (distaste for all the government BS that comes with being an employer) to emotional preference (I have little patience). But once, I took over a troubled company with forty-two employees. I made a whole bundle of dumb mistakes, most resulting from trying to actually follow the advice about management I read in management books. I also accomplished a lot. Under my direction, this "team" that had been woefully unproductive, manufacturing with quality control problems exceeding 50 percent, riddled with tardiness and absenteeism, turned things around. We cut quality control problems from the ungodly 50 percent of goods made to below 7 percent of goods made. Measured productivity doubled. Absenteeism and tardiness down to near zero. Before it was over, I helped unleash a few "champions" out of that group. I also "cut" a lot of them. Also, I learned a lot. I learned that you are better served by doing the opposite of what most books on management tell you to do. And I learned what Jimmy Johnson had learned elsewhere, in sports: that you MUST manage different people differently in order to get successful results.

Why "Management by Discrimination" Makes So Much Sense

In their book *Sacred Cows Make the Best Hamburgers,* Robert Kriegel and David Brundt observed that "it's nearly impossible to motivate individuals to change when your path is blocked by the sacred cow: treat everyone the same." They note that the idea of treating everybody the same is a remnant of the Judeo-Christian ethic of justice and the union agenda of equity in the workplace. These are anchors hung around a leader's neck. And this is still the most commonly taught, believed, and attempted approach to managing people today. The much more successful and, when logically analyzed, sensible approach is Jimmy Johnson's. In sync with Coach Johnson, these authors note that you can't effectively manage the superstar the same way you manage the journeyman, motivate creative talent the same way you motivate bookkeepers. Doing so stifles creativity, dedication, enjoyment of work, and psychic satisfaction. It creates energyless drones.

A longtime friend told me of the attack of the efficiency experts at his company. A big *Fortune* 500 corporation acquired the odd little manufacturing and direct sales company that was a cash cow. Then they sent in the high-priced consultants as the prelude to imposing some real management on this ragtag operation that was making nothing but money. The consultant tried to do the same time-and-motion studies on the inside sales reps as they did the manufacturing people. Unfortunately, this company's number one salesperson, by a big margin, was virtually immune to such analysis. He showed up some days at 7:00 A.M., other days after 10:00. He read the racing form and called his bookie. He took a coffee break after almost every call. He "wasted" incredible amounts of time on a woefully disorganized file system, wandering the halls, joking with the secretaries, even taking naps. However, when on the phone with a qualified prospect, he was, in direct sales parlance, a stone-cold killer. He rarely missed. So at the end of every month when all the dust settled, he outsold the others three or four to one. In an average month, he made the company about $50,000 net. Can you guess the end of this story?

The consultants went back to the executives in the *Fortune* 500 ivory tower and told them how completely disorganized, inefficient, and undisciplined these salespeople were—especially THIS salesman. They predicted tremendous increases in productivity if a tough manager went in and imposed some discipline on these people. So the *Fortune* 500 bigwigs dutifully dispatched one of their sales managers, a former career military officer, to whip the troops into shape. He laid down the law. Everybody will be treated exactly the same. Everybody will put in a nine-to-five day. Everybody will work forty-five minutes on the phones, fifteen minutes off. And so on. In very short order, the number one salesman walked and went to a competitor who, as IBM's Tom Watson once advised, had better sense than to try and force wild geese to fly in formation. In ninety days, sales dropped by nearly a third. Eventually, the *Fortune* 500 giant divested itself of this company for less than half of what they paid for it. Had they managed by discrimination rather than dictum, they'd have been a whole lot richer.

Zero Defects, Seeking Excellence, Quality Going in Circles, and All That Jazz

Here's another nifty management truth that isn't: the idea of "zero tolerance" for mistakes. A lot of companies went crazy in the eighties with quality control, quality circles, commitment to excellence, and zero tolerance, and they wound up with a bunch of scared, timid creatures incapable of innovation in their workplace. The message that was conveyed was: Don't you *dare* make a mistake.

If you've ever watched an NFL football team stuck starting their second- or third-string quarterback, coached by a conservative leader, you've seen some of the disastrous results of the "make no mistakes" plan. In these instances, the coach will sometimes instruct his quarterback: "Just don't lose the game for us." In other words, take no chances. No risks. Make no mistakes. Buddy Ryan tried to play it this way with the Arizona Cardinals for two years—telling his offensive coaches and QB to "not lose the game" and counting on his defense to keep the other team's scoring to a minimum. In two years of this, Ryan took a bad team and made its record much worse, destroyed its morale, drove away the fans, alienated the community, and wound up putting a totally demoralized, mistake-prone team on a field in a near empty stadium. This is why Ryan is no longer the head coach.

First of all, playing "not to lose" pits a fundamental psychological principle against you, your team, or your organization. That is, whatever a person or group of people think about most, focus on most, and/or fear most, they experience most. Call it self-fulfilling prophecy, visualization actualization, whatever. It happens. The fellow proudly wearing a brand-new silk tie—the most expensive one he's ever bought—who has a very important business meeting after lunch, who tells himself to be extra careful not to spill anything on himself at lunch, who worries about spilling something, is virtually guaranteed to spill and slop stuff on himself like never before.

When a business organization is burdened with the mandate of "don't make mistakes" and put in fear of making mistakes, everybody will inevitably wind up making plenty of mistakes. In fact, people become mistake prone.

How Saddam Hussein Manages New Ideas

Second, the no-mistakes mandate kills innovation. I frequently speak on programs where General Norman Schwarzkopf is one of the other speakers. I've heard his speech on leadership so many times I could probably give it, and I will steal one of his best stories here. General Schwarzkopf gives this insight into the character of Saddam Hussein. One day Saddam gathers all of his top lieutenants and aides-de-camp together for a little brainstorming session to look for a way to end the conflict with the United States short of war. One man, a close aide of Saddam's for many years, carefully, diplomatically suggests that the problem has become a personal spitting contest between Saddam and George Bush; that emotions, egos, "face," now preclude a resolution; and that the impasse and inexorable march toward war might best be broken if Saddam temporarily stepped down as president, let a different president lead negotiations and arrive at a resolution, then he could step aside and Saddam could resume power. Saddam took out his gun and shot this fellow dead. Then he said, "Who else has an idea?"

Third, the no-mistakes mandate fosters cover-one's-ass cover-ups. Unfortunately, mistakes, problems, and failures can be concealed only for so long. Eventually, ultimately, they surface, often after having gotten so bad they can no longer be solved. The demise of Richard Nixon's presidency was the result of an admit-no-mistakes philosophy and an environment of fear, where being the one caught screwing up was akin to being a traitor or incompetent, to be purged from the inner circle. Many political pundits and historians have suggested that had Richard Nixon been able to come forward early, quickly, and say, "We made a terrible mistake. We've burned all the tapes for national security reasons. And here are the steps I am taking to make certain such a thing never happens again," he would have finished his second term in office and had an opportunity to leave with dignity instead of in disgrace. I agree. I also think that a Nixonian atmosphere has prevailed in the Clinton administration with regard to Whitewater, "Travelgate," Ron Brown, and other scandals. As of this writing, it has not destroyed this presidency. Yet.

The contrarian approach is to make as many mistakes as possible, at as rapid a pace as possible, learning as much as possible from them, laughing about them, shrugging them off, and moving on. Entrepreneurial friends of mine call this "failing forward."

Of course, you want to do this as inexpensively as possible. You don't want to be wasteful or irresponsible. But on the other hand, being overly paranoid and uptight about being wrong means you never get to be really, really right either. Almost all really great achievements come from taking a chance.

There is also a very valid principle to keep in mind: In many situations, good enough is good enough. An argument FOR "zero defects" once advanced by a consultant in that field, Jeff Dewar of QCI International, goes like this: If things were done only 99.9 percent right, we'd have to accept:

One hour of unsafe drinking water every month.
Two unsafe plane landings every day at O'Hare in Chicago.

Sixteen thousand pieces of mail lost by the USPS every hour. Twenty thousand incorrect drug prescriptions a year.

The first thing I'd say to Mr. Dewar is that he is naive if he thinks we aren't living with such screwups. But more importantly, let's not get carried away. The Dewar argument holds up with airplane landings, for example, but does NOT hold up when applied, say, to eggs being fried in a diner, envelopes stuffed in a mailing house, or boxes of auto parts packed in a factory. An analysis of "zero defects" published in *Industry Week* magazine (September 20, 1993) noted that "some quality zealots may be tempted to forget the ancient law of diminishing returns. It is time, asserts a team of manufacturing experts at Corning, Inc., to address an important question: are there any limits to how far and fast a firm should push toward reducing defects in the product or process? Simply put, should 'zero defects' be everybody's goal? Probably not, contends Norman Edelson, new process development manager (and others) at Helsinki University of Technology. . . . It is becoming apparent that an exaggerated program of defect reduction may REDUCE a firm's competitiveness. . . . Advocates of continuous improvement sometimes imply that any activity to reduce variability is justified, no matter what the cost, or how meager the gains. We believe, on the contrary, that it is time to set some limits."

Even Tony Robbins became infatuated with preaching what the Japanese call "kaizan," meaning continuous and constant improvement, in search of excellence. But economic reality tells us that you can go broke applying kaizan in the wrong place, at the wrong time. A simple example: I spent a few years in the custom, spoken-word audiocassette manufacturing business, producing large quantities of recorded cassettes for speakers, seminar companies, churches, universities, and corporations. When I took over the company, its defect rate was in the double-digits. I brought it down to about 7 percent. But to go the rest of the way, to get from 7 percent to 0 percent defects, the cost would have required me to DOUBLE my prices, and I would have lost every single account if I did. That

7 percent differential just did not have that kind of marketplace value to anybody.

I find all sorts of situations where good enough is good enough. For example, I often tell "students" of mine who own small businesses to use my models and instructions to write their own sales letters rather than hiring me at my large fees and royalties to do it for them. Why? Certainly I could do it better—much better. But considering their limited usage, and the fact that they are in an industry or market where nobody else is using anything similar to the kind of materials I recommend, they will get more than satisfactory results with their own efforts even if they are 50 percent as effective as I might be. When you weigh all the factors, they are better off financially with "good enough is good enough" instead of the very best that money can buy.

Those who preach excellence at any cost, no matter what, may never have actually run a business or met a payroll. They are dangerously out of touch with reality.

CONTRARIAN SUCCESS STRATEGY:

If you play not to lose, you lose. To get great ideas, breakthroughs, and innovation you must accept, even embrace, mistakes and, if managing others, provide an environment where it is perfectly safe to make mistakes. Learn what you can from every goof-up, take steps to prevent repeating dumb mistakes, but beware the "excellence at any cost" attitude—it'll probably cost you more than it's worth. In today's downsized, lean 'n mean situations, a key managerial skill is compromise, knowing when it is best to settle for less than perfection.

CHAPTER 17

"If It Ain't Broke, Don't Fix It"— Unless You Want To

"If you're not Number One, I think you have to innovate."
—Lee Iacocca

If a company has doubled its profits every five years, how many things could possibly need fixing? That's where PepsiCo was in 1992, but CEO Wayne Calloway went about making changes as if sales were falling by half every five years. Long a soft-drink company by definition, Pepsi diversified its beverage business, adding Lipton iced tea in bottles, All Sport, an electrolyte drink, CrystalPepsi, and fruit juices. In the Frito-Lay Division, innovation is the name of the game, and the push was on to create better tasting products, new products, and low-fat and fat-free products. By trimming 1,800 executive jobs, getting lean n' mean, and rapidly introducing new products, they ultimately drove Anheuser-Busch's Eagle Snacks Division out of business. "The test of management," Calloway told *Fortune* magazine, "is the nerve to change."

But when is the time to change?

You have certainly heard "Don't rock the boat," "Let sleeping dogs lie," "If it ain't broke, don't fix it." Yet the people who make big things happen kick sleeping dogs awake with daring and impunity. There may be no better example of that than

Dallas Cowboys' owner Jerry Jones. He buys the team, fires a living legend, Tom Landry, cleans house, and hires a college coach untested in pro ball and viewed by many in pro ball as a loudmouth motivator with lots of bluster, little substance. After a massive rebuilding process and a terrible season, Johnson and team go to the Super Bowl two years back-to-back. The luster and glamour and status of Dallas as America's team is restored. They are bigger, badder, and, not incidentally, more profitable than ever before. In fact, this franchise is a money machine. Jones has managed to recover the $90 million cash and eliminate the debt he put up to buy the team and turned a financially troubled business into the most profitable team in the NFL. So, if it ain't broke—Jerry again shakes everything up all over again. Incredibly, he dumps Johnson and brings in another college coach, untested in pro ball, controversial in college, entirely out of coaching for years, and widely viewed as a motivational loudmouth. Worse, he is from Oklahoma, a sports "enemy" of Texas. Also, Jones takes on the entire NFL in a war over money, advertising, licensing, the entire revenue-sharing structure of the NFL. He deals to get that egotistical, arrogant so-and-so Deion Sanders, risking disrupting the chemistry of the whole team. And the team does struggle, but it still gets through the play-offs and again wins the Super Bowl. And is a bigger money machine than ever.

Jones is no stranger to controversy or high-wire risk taking. He made monster money in the 1970s in the energy industry when he followed the contrarian advice of a maverick geologist who insisted that oil and gas reserves could be found by drilling right between the dry holes on previously abandoned sites.

Is Jerry Jones nuts? Check his bank balance, then decide.

"Nothing stands still," Jerry Jones says. "You shouldn't ever wait to make changes."

Bigger Candles

If we had operated on "If it ain't broke, don't fix it," we'd all be lighting our houses with bigger candles, cleaning up after our horses with pooper scoopers out in our driveways. I'd be typing this manuscript on a manual typewriter. Our automobiles would not have antilock brakes or safety air bags. Our homes would not have central air or heat. Good grief, our television sets wouldn't have remote controls! All progress and innovation, from the important to the comparatively trivial but convenient, are based on constructive dissatisfaction with the status quo.

Two-thirds of the companies profiled in Tom Peters's *In Search of Excellence* in 1982 have underperformed the S&P 500 over the last decade. Several have gone belly-up, at least one in an embarrassing spectacle. So, instead of preaching excellence, Tom Peters has made a living and then some these last few years by getting in business leaders' faces and daring them to shake everything up, turn things upside down, question every premise, create chaos, and reinvent their businesses as many times as possible, as fast as possible. In his book *The Tom Peters Seminar*, he celebrates companies led by people willing to encourage chaos. And he asks the provocative question: How do we systematically go about forgetting what we "know" before it suffocates us?

You've been told "knowledge is power." But I'll bet nobody's told you that "too much knowledge all too often disembowels the powerful."

Sometimes you CAN know too darned much. At age forty plus, I find myself constantly wrestling with a problem I certainly never had at age twenty plus: I know so much, and have, in so many cases, "been there, done that," that I am quick to impose the outcomes I experienced from certain ideas and efforts on others as perfect predictions of their outcomes. Nothing could be further from the truth. Often, ignorance, determination, enthusiasm, and youth will create a very positive result from basically doing the same thing that has previously proven disastrous. Times change. Circumstances change. People change. Everything changes every day. What was true yesterday may very well be false tomorrow. Excess knowledge too often breeds cynicism.

Media mogul Barry Diller shocked all his peers in the entertainment industry when he took the helm at QVC, the home shopping network. Why on earth would a man of Diller's stature lower himself to be in the cubic-zirconia-and-stuffed-doll-selling business? In a 1993 interview, quoted in Tom Peters's book, Diller expressed his excitement at coming into a new industry and environment with "a clean slate," where you get to "screw things up" a lot and act on instinct. He also sagely observed that it's very difficult to sustain that freshness. He talked about getting sophisticated, inundated with research and information, indoctrinated in the norms of the business; "captured by the process."

I think it is extremely important to avoid being captured by the process. A good discipline is to constantly ask: What happens if we do the OPPOSITE of what we are doing now?

How I Changed the Way My Clients Advertise by Doing the Opposite

I was indoctrinated, like most people in the advertising business, with the traditional approach of advertising the product. If your client manufactures bowling balls, you advertise his bowling ball. If your client sells insurance, you advertise the insurance product or the company. But observing "personal ads" changed my entire approach.

If you take a look at a personal ad, it does advertise the "product" a bit. But more than that, it advertises FOR the person the advertiser wants to attract. I saw this as the opposite of all traditional advertising. What would happen if, instead of advertising the product, we advertised FOR the utopian customer or client desired by and well matched to the advertiser? The result is what I call "pure lead generation advertising." Let me give you a simple example. Let's say you sell financial products, like annuities, perfect for owners of family businesses who are personally nearing retirement age. Here's a pure lead generation ad aimed at just that person:

WARNING For Owners of Family Businesses Who Are Personally Nearing Retirement Age

The IRS has *you* in its sights! There are seven giant financial mistakes made by most family business founders/owners as they near retirement, that can cost you $10,000 to $100,000 or more. Even many financial advisors, CPA's, etc. are unaware of these mistakes or negligent about protecting clients from them. My Free Report: *Seven Tax Secrets for Family Business Owners* reveals how you can structure succession, asset transfers, retirement income, etc. to pay the absolute legal minimum in taxes. For details and a complimentary copy of my Free Report, sent by mail, confidentially to your office or home, call my free recorded message: 000/000-0000.

For clarity's sake, one other example: Assume you run a women's dress shop, featuring top-name fashions, especially business attire, at 30 percent to 50 percent discounts from department store prices. Again, instead of advertising the products or the store, the contrarian approach is to advertise FOR the desired customer, like this:

ATTENTION Career & Business Women: How to Get Top Name Fashions & Business Attire at 30% to 50% Discounts—Without Waiting for "Sales"

You work hard for your money. You must dress "up," better than most, to present the right image for your career. This challenges you to be smart about money. Now, there is a new way for you to buy current, seasonal business and casual fashions, including designer names, at as much as 50% *off* the typical department store price. For confidential details, call my Free Recorded Message: 000/000-0000.

How well does this approach work? I have clients in over sixty-eight different categories of business who have come to rely on it for acquiring new customers, clients, accounts, or patients at a much lower cost than from traditional advertising methods.

Niche Markets Become Traps

I am a big believer in "niche marketing" or niche exploitation.

I have many clients and a few joint venture partners whom I've taught to make fortunes by exploiting their connections to specialty, niche markets: a successful carpet cleaner selling advertising kits, marketing information, software, other business opportunities, and seminars to other carpet cleaners; a landscaper doing the same with the landscaping industry; a Certified Financial Planner doing the same thing with that industry; and so on.

The biggest virtue of attacking a niche market is minimal waste. All the media are targeted and well read, so you can target your message. The biggest drawback is speed of saturation. Reaching a double-digit market share can require only a few months and you can hit the wall of diminishing returns at 30 percent to 50 percent market share in only a year or two. So there is an absolute certainty that what works will stop working purely because of the finite number of reasonably responsive prospects for it to work on. To extend your life selling to a niche market, you have to fix what is not yet broken but definitely will be in the very near future.

For All the Wrong Reasons

A lot of things continue to be done the way they've always been done, mostly because nobody has the guts to ask Why. Here's a perfect example:

Of course, in our homes, we've abandoned the wringer washing machine. (My grandmother had one.) Drying clothes on the line has been replaced with the clothes dryer. But still . . . this is a favorite Zig story of mine: A young married couple is hosting a New Year's Day dinner for the first time. Hubby is helping out in the kitchen and sees his wife hack off both ends of the ham. "Why'd you do that?" he asks. She says: Because Momma always did. So he goes out to the living room and asks Momma why she always cuts the ends of the ham. "Because my Momma always did." So he calls Grandma up at the nursing home, gets her to the phone, and says, "My wife is cutting the ends off the ham. She says your daughter always did. She says you always did. So I'm calling to find out why."

"I don't know why those damn fool girls are doing it," says the old lady. "I always did it cuz we only had the one pan and it was too small for the ham."

I caught a consulting client once—all his sales reps were filling out four-part carbonless forms. But the form hadn't been changed in three years. During that time, the whole computer system had been overhauled twice, so that now, only two copies of the form were being used, and two were thrown away by the clerks doing the data input. But everything was done the same old way, without question. If you go through your whole operation, I wonder if you'll find any ends-cut-off-the-ham stories?

On the other hand, change just for the sake of change is much less desirable than change motivated by compelling reasons, initiated quickly. These days, in most businesses, there are plenty of pressures and opportunities that demand change. Be smart instead of stubborn; test new strategies rather than clinging to old ones.

Ego is an interesting force. Ego can cause a person to defend and protect his way of doing things long after they should have or could have been improved and changed for the better. Ego can also cause someone to make wholesale changes just to flex his muscles and demonstrate his authority. Neither extreme is productive.

Recently, I had a client completely revamp a particular procedure for selling and fulfilling orders at large trade shows. It worked just fine the way it was but, as the new man on the block, the new vice-president, decided to change it all around for increased efficiency. Turns out he was right about his way being more efficient. Unfortunately, his way also reduced sales by nearly 15 percent.

So, you shouldn't throw all caution out the window. You have to frankly analyze your motivations for pushing change. But by and large, things are better shaken up than left alone.

CONTRARIAN SUCCESS STRATEGY:

If it ain't broke, challenge it anyway. Ask bizarre questions. Shake things up. Try doing the opposite and see if that works even better. Refuse to let experience block experimentation. Things have changed since yesterday—have you?

Some of My Favorite Contrarians

Here's an eclectic group of contrarians, past and present, who have impressed me for one reason or another.

Dr. D. D. Palmer

In 1895, D. D. Palmer began practicing and teaching chiropractic. In short, chiropractic is a health-care discipline based on the philosophy that humans are endowed with the capability of enjoying lifetime optimum health; that Nature can provide that if not interfered with; and that certain kinds of injuries, stress, and the like can cause misalignment of the spine blocking the natural energy flow. Chiropractic philosophy is that health comes from within. Today, science has validated chiropractic in many ways, and the American Medical Association lost a major lawsuit when they were found to be in violation of the Sherman Antitrust Act, engaged in a deliberate conspiracy to restrict and ultimately exterminate the chiropractic profession. But in its early days, D. D. Palmer, his son B. J. Palmer, and those joining them in practicing and promoting chiropractic were prosecuted, arrested, and imprisoned. B. J. Palmer and those who have followed him have courageously taken on the medical establishment and the entire medical model of treating every malady with drugs or surgery. The Palmers launched the greatest contrarian health-care movement in the history of the world.

It's worthy of mention, by the way, that chiropractic is booming and is bigger than ever, as is the entire "alternative" and "holistic" health field. Consider one of the field's most popular spokespersons, Deepak Chopra, author of the best-selling book *Ageless Body, Timeless Mind* and a couple "big" books since, a favorite of Oprah Winfrey, a darling of PBS-TV. But not a favorite of the medical community. The kindest interpretation of one critic: "He's just ripping people off for a couple hundred bucks for tapes." This entire field or industry or movement, whatever term you prefer, led by people like Chopra, is contrarian to the medical establishment.

Ayn Rand

Ayn Rand is one of my heroes. Hopefully you've read Ayn Rand's novels, notably *Atlas Shrugged.* If not, please do. If you haven't done so in the last few years, reread them. *Atlas Shrugged* sold over 1.2 million copies in its first six years of publication and, of course, has continued to sell as a "classic." In its time, it was the most admired and the most damned and reviled best-seller on the shelf. That any work of fiction could ever create such incredible controversy, enthusiasm, and serious following is amazing. Ayn Rand described herself as in profound disagreement with modern American politics, economics, attitudes toward sex, art, religion, and business. "I am challenging the cultural traditions of 2,000 years," she once told an interviewer. And that she did. By daring to offend millions, Rand sold millions of copies of her novels via a word-of-mouth firestorm, launched a philosophical movement, and achieved fame and fortune. *The New Yorker* magazine noted that "few American novelists have had the force or desire to turn readers into disciples, to shape political or religious or moral convictions."

Ayn Rand identified herself as "the chief writer of 'propaganda fiction.'"

Incidentally, Allan Greenspan, chairman of the Federal Reserve during the Carter, Reagan, Bush, and Clinton administrations, is a passionate devotee of Ayn Rand's philosophies, although many would argue some of his actions and his political allies are in conflict. Ayn Rand's novels were reportedly widely read within the Reagan White House.

There is a current resurgence of interest in Rand, now fourteen years after her death. Her books continue to sell over four hundred thousand copies each year. There is an Ayn Rand Institute and an annual "Objectivism Conference."

Bill Bennett

I have had the privilege of appearing at a number of seminar events with former secretary of education, former drug czar, and author of *The Book of Virtues,* William Bennett.

Bill Bennett was once a Democrat; he is now a Republican. He claims the Democratic party changed more than he did.

At a time when the prevailing trends have been to increase and emphasize gratuitous sex and violence in movies, television programs, and music, with each new release pushing the envelope farther than the next, and when the prevailing attitude among media, business, political, and entertainment industry elite has been that this equals sophistication, and to oppose it or criticize it is to reveal yourself as an unsophisticated, out-of-step bumpkin or dangerous censor, Bill Bennett dared to speak out against this denigration of culture. He first took on rap music, rife with violence, vicious and dehumanizing treatment of women, incitement of violence against law enforcement officers, and romancing of drug use and casual sex. When no one else would, Bill Bennett spoke out against these lyrics, the entertainers who performed them, and the companies that profited from them. He dared music industry executives to defend these products; the executives hid. He dared the executives of the biggest music company putting out this music to read the lyrics of their own recordings aloud; they refused. He marshaled public opinion, took on media critics, and ultimately pressured a giant music and entertainment corporation to divest itself of their rap music artists and products. In doing so, he put the spotlight of truth on these products and brought the critical attention of who knows how many parents to what their kids were listening to.

You can be opposed to censorship, as I am, and a militant defender of the Constitution, as I am, and still feel, as I do, that companies have an obligation to society to draw the line at what they will do for money somewhere short of popularizing rape and murder.

Bill Bennett's leadership is also responsible for the television industry's establishment of a rating system for TV programs similar to that of the movie industry, to assist parents in policing what their children watch and are not permitted to watch. It is yet to be seen how actually useful this proves to be, but the entertainment industry mostly fought it as long as they could while most parents favored it.

Time-Warner executives have described Bill as "In-your-face insulting." Writing in *The New Yorker,* Michael Kelly calls Bill Bennett "an opportunist . . . something of a bully, an overbearing ex-jock who traffics in confrontation and intimidation . . . rude . . . a Barnumesque sensationalist . . . a light-fingered popularizer of others' ideas." But by all accounts, even those of the opposition, Bennett works hard to practice the virtues he preaches and may be without significant skeletons in his closet. Personally, I am convinced he passionately believes in his positions and can be trusted to tell you exactly what he believes, regardless of the popularity or unpopularity or acceptance or criticism of the position. He does not alter his positions to suit the audience of the moment, a rather refreshing virtue in and of itself.

He is far from always careful or polite in expressing his views. About former Surgeon General Dr. Jocelyn Elders and her advocacy of teaching masturbation and distributing free condoms in public schools, for example, Bill was quoted as saying, "Standard Jocelyn Elders. She said this kind of garbage everyday. The woman was a nitwit."

About criticism, Bill says, "Criticism doesn't matter. It keeps you alert. It keeps you busy. But it doesn't matter in the long run. When I became secretary of education, I had forty-five editorials saying I should resign, all written within my first three weeks, because of my controversial positions. I remember reading them at night and feeling depressed. But I got up in the morning and went to work. And that's what you do even if heavily criticized; you go to work. I have my commitments, convictions, and I believe I'm doing something worthwhile. If you believe in what you are doing and have reason to believe in what you are doing, you do it regardless of the way the wind is blowing at the moment."

Walt Disney

The next time you visit Disneyland, in Anaheim, or World, in Orlando, know that there was not a single expert anywhere who believed in Walt's vision. In 1953, mostly to try and satisfy possible financial backers, Walt commissioned researchers at Stanford University to do a feasibility study of his plans for Disneyland. These researchers visited all the major amusement parks in the United States and Europe. At the 1953 annual convention of the owners of amusement parks, the researchers had a late-night session with the owners, where everybody looked at Walt's plans. The feedback was unanimous: It was a foolish idea. Not enough ride capacity. Too much of the park was non–revenue producing. The newfangled rides would cost too much to maintain. Every expert argued against Walt's single-entry concept. Fortunately, the Stanford group's final report did contain some encouraging information, such as the track record of the San Diego Zoo's unusual success at maintaining year-round traffic. But on par, any sensible businessperson would have turned his back on the entire idea. Walt simply insisted that he was not creating another amusement park. He was doing something different, so their dire warnings didn't matter.

In the development of Disneyland, Walt also went contrary to the obvious; instead of hiring people experienced in buying, building, installing, or designing amusement park attractions, he assembled a team of six men experienced only as motion picture art directors—the people responsible for creation of movie sets.

Tony Bennett

I'm somewhat distraught in admitting that there is not a single musical group or performer seen regularly on MTV that I like, with the exception of Tony Bennett.

At age sixty-seven, after forty years in the music business, still doing exactly what he has always done, Tony Bennett suddenly is hip and hot all over again. Even though his style is dated, his standard performing attire is a tux or a suit, he has won a whole new following of twenty- and thirty-year-olds. Appeared on MTV. Sung a duet with k. d. lang. Even appeared in person at concerts with the Lemonheads, Red Hot Chili Peppers and, gulp, Porno for Pyros. The twenty-year-old lead singer of a local Toronto rock band, waiting in line at a Tony Bennett autograph session at a record store, said, "He's, like, pure star. Real cool."

To be sure, Tony owes some of this to the very savvy promotional efforts directed by his forty-year-old son, Danny, who took charge of his dad's career in the mid-1980s. Some must be attributed to the fact that, throughout his entire career, Tony Bennett has never given in to record company pressure to change his style, record faddish music or music he didn't like, or try to be something other than himself. There is a new appreciation among relatively young fans for stars who have been very consistent and true to themselves throughout their entire careers, like Bennett, Johnny Cash, and Frank Sinatra.

Along the way, Tony walked away from his long-running, lucrative contract with Columbia Records in the 1970s when they demanded that he record more "current" songs. "They wanted me to sing Janis Joplin," Tony Bennett said ruefully. "I told them: 'You do it.' " He came back to Sony Columbia in 1986, this time on his own terms, in control.

Danny Bennett's contrarian marketing strategy for the Tony Bennett renaissance was simple: He said, "Let's have the marketing fit the artist, instead of the other way around." As for the product: "Don't change a thing." No electronic synthesizers, no wild wardrobes, no contrived songs with great crossover potential. Tony could keep being Tony, doing what he did best, and Danny would go and find a new, appreciative audience. "You just put him in front of enough people, they're gonna get it and it doesn't matter what age they are," insisted Danny. He has been proven right. Tony Bennett has become a hit with the nose rings and oversize T-shirt, Gen X crowd without in any way changing himself or his "product" to try to appeal to them. That's about as contrarian as you can get.

Booker T. Washington

You can find Booker T. Washington's autobiography, published in 1901, buried on a dusty shelf at your library. You'll probably be surprised at what an inspiring, ahead-of-its-time exhortation for self-reliance and entrepreneurship it is.

Booker T. Washington was no different from most blacks of his time; he was born into slavery and grew up illiterate. But unlike many, through determination and sacrifice, he secured an education. He made himself into one of the most influential speakers, leaders, and motivators in American history—and he taught blacks the contrarian way to lift themselves up out of poverty. After Reconstruction, ex-slaves were eager to distance themselves from manual labor, which they regarded as a link to their past slavery. Washington taught that all work, no matter how lowly, was a God-given opportunity to build character and acquire necessary skills and disciplines. He preached a free market philosophy, urging blacks to be entrepreneurial and to create service businesses, doing those things people most wanted done, taking pride in doing them well, and using them to create financial success. Washington also scoffed at political solutions to discrimination or poverty, instead insisting that blacks had to create their own prosperity and gain the respect of others by succeeding in the free market. He was fiercely opposed by both the NAACP and white supremacist groups.

Today, black conservatives like syndicated columnist Thomas Sowell and popular radio personality Ken Hamblin carry on the Booker T. Washington contrarian tradition, insisting that Washington cannot cure poverty with handouts or eliminate racism with legislation, and urging blacks to embrace the free enterprise system.

Columbo

When William Link and Richard Levinson brought the rumpled, raincoated Columbo to television, they violated every imaginable rule of detective shows and, pretty much, of TV in general. Columbo is a thinking person's detective. Some of the episodes, such as the one with Louis Jordan as the killer restaurant critic, were downright artistic. Imagine—an hourlong detective show with no car chases, virtually no violence, no gunplay, no fistfights, the detective never being hit over the head in the dark ... incredible. The hero completely faithful and in love with his wife, polite even to the villains, sartorially handicapped, quietly bemused by man's inhumanity to man, slow and patient ... remarkable. But enormously successful' and sadly missed. I cannot imagine pitching this idea to any television or movie executives.

Bill Maher

I like Bill because he created a political talk show for television that breaks every known rule for such shows and has been appearing on The Comedy Channel, where no serious talk belongs. He calls his show *Politically Incorrect,* "something like the McLaughlin Report on acid." If you haven't seen it, its premise is simple: Bill invites a group of guests on, sets up a timely topic, and turns everybody loose on that topic and on one another. That's not much different from McLaughlin, *Crossfire,* or the Sunday-morning Brinkley. The big difference is the guests invited into the debates. For example, death penalty pros and cons argued by Roseanne, Quentin Tarantino, and Senator Arlen Specter. The guest list has included *Jeopardy*'s host Alex Trebek, political author David Halberstam, Guns N' Roses lead guitarist Slash, Russian pundit Vladimir Posner, Joan Rivers, LA District Attorney Ira Reiner, Kato Kaelin, Adrienna Huffington, Sandra Bernhard, Sam Donaldson, and basketball player John Salley. This is a show that should not work but does, usually brilliantly.

Maher says about himself, "People who don't know me well hate me and they always have. I used to worry about that, but I can't anymore. I make a rotten first-through-ninth impression. And I don't warm up to people quickly." Given that, Maher is probably a person who shouldn't be successful in the schmooze-schmooze entertainment industry. But he is. By the time this book is published, his show should be following *Nightline* on most ABC stations. Enjoy!

AUTHOR'S AFTERWORD

Indulge me in a favorite story . . .

The wise old rabbi, on his deathbed, has had gathered around him his rabbinical students for the deathwatch. His students are lined up alongside the bed, the best and brightest of all the students at his head, the next best student next, and so on, down to the dullard at the foot of the bed. As it becomes increasingly apparent that the revered old rabbi is taking his last breaths, the number one student leans over and whispers, "Master, before you leave us, would you please, finally, simply share with us: What is the true meaning of life?"

Summoning a bit of strength, the rabbi raises his head slightly off the pillow and gasps, "Life is like a river."

The student turns to the next brightest student at his side and whispers, "The Master says life is like a river. Pass it on." That student turns to the next brightest student and says, "The Master says life is like a river. Pass it on." And so the wisdom is passed from student to student to student, until it is whispered to the dullest student, standing all the way down at the foot of the bed. He says: "What does he mean—life is like a river? What does that mean?"

So it is passed back up the line: What does the Master mean life is like a river? The dullard wants to know.

The best student stops it. He says, "I am not going to disturb the Master with such a question. It is obvious. A river runs deep. Life is deep. A river has twists and turns. Life has twists and turns. Sometimes the river's water is clear, other times murky. Life is sometimes clear, sometimes murky. Pass that back down to the dullard."

And so that message is passed from student to student to, finally, the dunce of the class. But he is insistent. "Listen," he says, "I don't want to know what that smart aleck thinks the Master means. I want to know what the Master means. Life is like a river. Exactly what does he mean by that?"

So the dunce's demand is passed back up the line.

Annoyed, grudgingly, the number one student again leans over the dying rabbi. "Master, I beg your forgiveness, but the dunce of our class has demanded that I ask you—what do you mean 'life is like a river'?"

Marshaling his last bit of energy, the wise old rabbi again raises his head and says, "Okay, so it's not like a river," shrugs his shoulders, and dies.

The point is that there's not a whole lot of difference between most dogma and dog poop.

Had the rabbi died before answering the dunce's "dumb" question, his "Life is like a river" statement might very well have birthed an entire dogmatic philosophy of life. His loyal disciples would have gone out into the world to spread the Master's wisdom. Books would have been written. Tapes recorded. And so on.

If this book has done nothing else for you, I hope it has inspired you to be damned contrarian about accepting somebody else's one and only right way to do a thing or anybody else's carved-in-cement wisdom. Challenge it all. Don't be afraid to ask the "dumb" question. Never be intimidated by an authority figure. Scrape the dogma from your boot and go make things happen YOUR way.

Dan S. Kennedy

ACKNOWLEDGMENTS

This book would never have been completed without the efforts and assistance of my research assistant, Theresa Harper, my wife and chief manuscript fixer upper, Carla, and my editors Deborah Brody and Jennifer Moore at Penguin.

Notices

There is an inherent problem with an anecdote-driven book like this one. Most books, including this one, hit the bookstore shelves a year or so after leaving the authors' hands. It is inevitable that some of the information will no longer be current. Some of the people profiled in this book will have gone on to even greater or more memorable accomplishments. Some may even have tripped, stumbled, disgraced themselves. All people are flawed, as you very well know. I do not think any of this negates the value of the stories included here and the principles they demonstrate.

Communication with the Author

I welcome your letters or fax communication, and will be happy to send you a free catalog describing all of my books, cassettes, home study courses, seminars, and newsletter. Write to: Dan Kennedy, 5515 N. 7th Street #5–149, Phoenix, Arizona 85014 or fax 602/269-3113. Schedule permitting, I am also available for speaking engagements or consulting assignments.

Other Books by the Author Available in Most Bookstores or via 1-800-223-7180

1. *How to Make Millions with Your Ideas: An Entrepreneur's Guide.* Published by Plume/Penguin.
2. *The No B.S., No Holds Barred, Take No Prisoners, Kick Butt & Makes Tons Of Money Business Success Book.* Published by Self-Counsel Press.
3. *The No B.S. Sales Success Book.* Published by Self-Counsel Press.
4. *The No B.S. Time Management Book for Super Busy Entrepreneurs.* Published by Self-Counsel Press.
5. *The Ultimate Marketing Plan.* Published by Adams Media.
6. *The Ultimate Sales Letter.* Published by Adams Media.